# WHAT OTHERS ARE SAYING...

"A beautiful work from a compelling author, *Treasures of the Believing Heart* can be a powerful beacon of light for any heart that knows what it is looking for."

—Tim Newcomb, Author and Attorney

With the skill of a cartographer, Rich Wessenberg, in Treasure of a Believing Heart, maps a clear path to a closer walk with God."

R. Vigil
Heartist and Master Teacher and Researcher
2000 Milken Family Foundation
Teacher of the Year, Cheyenne, WY

Rich Wessenberg incorporates his extensive knowledge of scripture and deep faith in God to lead the reader, step by step, to a realization that the treasures of a believing heart are contained in the Bible. Scripture quotations are used through-out the book to illustrate the "Law of Believing".

Carol Holland, Col, ret, USAF, Cheyenne, WY

As a sales person, this is a must read. Treasures of the Believing Heart is definitely a book I will refer to over and over. Rich is able to take every day work situations and remind us the benefits of staying true to our core values. This book is filled with valuable resources to help keep your believing heart strong. I will definitely recommend to my friends and colleagues.

-Sheryl Martin

# TREASURES

*of the*

# BELIEVING
# HEART

# TREASURES

*of the*

# BELIEVING HEART

RICH WESSENBERG

TATE PUBLISHING
AND ENTERPRISES, LLC

Published by Tate Publishing & Enterprises, LLC
127 E. Trade Center Terrace | Mustang, Oklahoma 73064 USA
1.888.361.9473 | www.tatepublishing.com

Tate Publishing is committed to excellence in the publishing industry. The company reflects the philosophy established by the founders, based on Psalm 68:11,
*"The Lord gave the word and great was the company of those who published it."*

Book design copyright © 2013 by Tate Publishing, LLC. All rights reserved.
*Cover design by Rodrigo Adolfo*
*Interior design by Jake Muelle*

Published in the United States of America

ISBN: 978-1-62902-046-4
1. Religion / General
2. Religion / Christian Life / General
13.12.18

# TABLE OF CONTENTS

# PREFACE

The purpose of this book is to inspire readers to seriously consider the good treasures of God's Word, the Bible. Proving that out of all the treasures in this world used to build the believing heart, the Bible has the best. Only the Bible can take you inside the believing heart, and reveal the real treasures of success and failure. Making the Bible, far and away the greatest self-help book ever written. However, the Bible is much more than a book of self-help, it is the Word of life. Once this truth is understood, then the Bible becomes a book from God written especially just for you, to help build your believing heart.

> For where your treasure is, there will your heart be also.
>
> Luke 12:34

*Treasures of the Believing Heart* is written with 2 Timothy 2:15 first and foremost in mind. Being an honest workman of the scripture, who is not to be ashamed and rightly dividing the Word of truth, is the very essence of this book.

> Study to shew thyself approved unto God, a workman that needeth not to be ashamed, rightly the word of truth.
>
> 2 Timothy 2:15

This book was made possible by my wife, Terri Wessenberg, and others who helped and encouraged its completion. It is dedicated to my children, Sarah and Stephen Wessenberg and all those who commit to building their believing hearts with the good treasure of God's Word, and finishing their course by living by believing.

# CHAPTER 1

# BECOMING THE WISEMAN

The greatest treasures you're ever going to find are the good treasures of the believing heart. No one should go through life without them. When found, they become the most precious of jewels and the most sought after of riches. Your life depends on them.

Life is spiritual and meant to be lived by believing. From the time we are born, until the time of death, the believing heart decides who we become. Like the rudder of a ship, it sets the course of life. Every course is a representative of spiritual power, which is energized believing. Most importantly, what is believed becomes a treasure of the believing heart, determining the kind of spiritual power energized into this world. This is the compelling spiritual nature of the believing heart. It's spiritual truth that is beyond the knowledge of this world. Only truth can separate the spiritual power at work in the believing heart. Everyone is affected by spiritual truth. It unites us all. Religion and politics separate believing hearts. Good treasures of the believing heart unite by a spiritual understanding that goes below the surface of what is right and wrong. Spiritual truth gets to the heart of every matter.

The believing heart impacts life all the time. It begins at each waking moment of the day, initiating the course of believing. Going unknown and undetected, it continues throughout each day. Concerns arise when courses are disrupted, diverted or prematurely ended. Life goes on and the believing heart remains incomplete like an unfinished puzzle. Missing are the pieces of truth. The pieces of truth specially designed for the believing heart to become whole.

> For the word of God *is* quick [biblically, quick means alive] and powerful, and sharper than any two edged sword, piercing even to the dividing asunder of soul and spirit, and of the joints and marrow, and *is* a discerner of the thoughts and intents of the heart.
>
> Hebrews 4:12

This verse from the Bible tells of pieces of truth that are for the believing heart. The Bible has words from God that are alive and powerful. This is a great foundational truth of believing. These are words that can separate soul from spirit. These words give critical examination of the believing heart and its course of believing. Words that when believed, energize the power of God. These are the good treasures of the believing heart.

> It is the spirit that quickened [biblically quickened means alive]; the flesh profited nothing: the words that *I* speak unto you, *they* are spirit, and *they* are life.
>
> John 6:63

The believing heart becomes whole by words that are spirit and life. This is always the first need of the believing heart. Once met, life flows in its natural order.

> And ye shall know the truth, and the truth shall make you free."
>
> John 8:32

The believing heart is designed, engineered, and functions best when words of truth are built within it. Words of truth have spirit and life in them. These are words that come from God and bring real freedom. Only one book in the whole world claims to be God's Word. That book is the Bible. The Bible has the words especially designed to fuel the believing heart. The Bible reveals the truth about believing, the believing heart, and the spiritual power that energizes it! The Bible is the only book that specifically addresses the believing heart desiring to live by believing. Once the Bible's treasures fill the believing heart, then the course of believing can be set by God.

> There hath no temptation taken you but such as is common to man: but God *is* faithful, Who will not suffer you to be tempted above that ye are able; but will with the temptation also make a way to escape, that ye may be able to bear *it*.
>
> 1 Corinthians 10:13

The Bible unveils the thoughts and intents of the believing heart, revealing its courses of believing. God's escape routes lead to freedom and life. Everything else eventually leads to captivity and death.

Only two spiritual courses exist in this world for the journey of life. Educating the believing heart on how to live by believing is the purpose of the Bible. Unfortunately, the believing heart can become its own worst enemy. Appreciating God doesn't always come naturally.

> Beloved I wish above all things that thou mayest prosper and be in health, even as thy soul prospereth.
>
> 3John 1:2

Above all things, God wants our lives to be on a course of prosperity and good health. This is how life is meant to be. All the problems in life begin and end with the kind of treasures found in the believing heart. Once fear, failure, and disappointment develop, little room is left for anything else. Recognizing God's goodness is the first step to escape an unprofitable course of believing. Only the goodness of God can change the believing heart.

> Now unto Him That is able to do exceeding abundantly above all that we ask or think, according to the power that worketh[biblically, worketh means energize] in us,
>
> Ephesians 3:20

God is able to do exceeding abundantly above all that we ask or think. What this really means is that the greatest course of believing found in this world cannot be compared to God's power working in us. Even if you spent your entire life trying to think how great God's course of believing could be, the Bible is saying that God is able to do exceeding abundantly above all you could ask or think! It truly is the best course of life! The only real question is how to change our courses from this world to his? Ephesians 3:20 explains his course as conditional, "according to the power that worketh in us." This means that certain biblical truths must first be applied. Since the times of Adam and Eve, this truth was understood and practically applied on a daily basis. It was the primary way of living life, even over bread and water. Biblically, this course of life is called living by believing. Living by believing is how the power of God works in us as we believe. This truth is seen throughout the Bible. Jesus mastered these truths and this is how he was able to help others. Mark 9:23-27 is a great example of this great truth of life.

> Jesus said unto him, "If thou canst believe, all things *are* possible to him that believeth."
>
> Mark 9:23

Jesus made these comments to a father who requested help for his chronically ill son. He recognized imprisoned believing and offered an escape. This father was brought to the crossroads of believing. There are only two ways you can go. Continue on with the course that has brought him to this destination or try something new.

> And straightway the father of the child cried out, and said with tears, "Lord, I believe; help Thou mine unbelief."
>
> Mark 9:24

Incredibly, this father cries out with tears, "LORD, I *believe; help Thou mine unbelief.*" This father recognized the limitations that handcuffed his believing and he wanted freedom! Help for unbelief is how the believing heart escapes an unprofitable course of believing! Mark 9:25-27 tells how this father received help for his unbelief and his son was healed. He honestly reached out for help and believed that God would heal his son. It's an example of how destiny becomes changed when the course of believing becomes changed. When an unprofitable course of believing becomes a profitable course.

Getting help for unbelief is the first step everyone takes to God's way and escape from unprofitable courses of believing! Once this journey begins, then expectations increase. Understanding what lies ahead becomes significantly important both in this world and in the next world to come. When it comes to receiving the power of God into our lives, there are two ends of the spectrum. On one end, God is able to do exceedingly abundantly above all we ask or think. At the other end, God promises to meet our need. At a minimum we can expect God to meet our need but this doesn't limit him from going over and above what we can ask or think.

> But my God shall supply all your need according
> to His riches in glory by Christ Jesus.
>
> Philippians 4:19

Historically, the Bible has captured and recorded some of the lives of those who lived by believing. God expects those who desire to live by believing to learn from these examples. Biblical examples represent spiritual courses of believing, revealing the kind of treasures found in the believing heart and the spiritual power they energized into this world. Once this truth is understood then the Bible becomes authored by God and written just for you.

> Shew me Thy ways, O Lord; Teach me Thy paths.
>
> Psalm 25:4

Are you ready for God's ways? Our way is comfortable since it's the only course we know. If we are willing to consider God's ways, the Bible says God will teach us his ways to help our unbelief. The courses of this world at their best have limitations of what is possible. They contain pitfalls, snares, curves which eventually lead to one way streets, with no way out. In contrast, God's courses of believing lead to a life where all things are possible; there are ways to escape and included is eternal life.

The twelve apostles of Jesus Christ were an example of living by believing. Men like Peter, John and Luke made up this special group. Together, they began their journey to build their believing hearts under Jesus' guidance.

> And the apostles said unto the Lord, "Increase our faith." [Biblically the word faith in this usage is believing and is many times translated as faith throughout the Bible]
>
> Luke 17:5

The twelve apostles watched Jesus live by believing and they wanted more of what he had. They wanted to increase their believing. As their journey was beginning, they realized that believing was the great key for the power of God to work in their lives. Jesus did not disappoint them. He taught them how to increase their believing.

> And the LORD said, "If ye had faith as a grain of mustard seed, ye might say unto this sycamine tree, "Be thou plucked up by the root, and be thou planted in the sea; and it should obey you.
>
> Luke 17:6

On the surface, this response doesn't make a lot of sense. However, below the surface, spiritually, it does. Jesus was teaching how the spiritual nature of believing works in the believing heart using a literal example. Biblically, this truth is known as the law of believing. The law of believing is a great treasure of the believing heart. Anyone who has lived by believing knows its importance to all life. Romans, chapter 3 is the one place in the Bible where the law of believing is specifically stated.

> To declare, I *say*, at this time his righteousness: that he might be just, and the justifier of him which believeth in Jesus.
>
> Where *is* boasting then? It is excluded. By what law? Of works? Nay: but by the law of faith.
>
> Romans 3:26,27

The law of believing is a spiritual law created by God. It's how spiritual power enters into this world. Mark 11:22-24 is another great example of the law of believing.

> And Jesus answering saith unto them, "have faith in God.
>
> For verily I say unto you, That whosoever shall say unto this mountain, Be thou removed, and be thou cast into the sea; and shall not doubt in his heart, but shall believe that those things which he saith shall come to pass he shall have whatsoever he saith.
>
> Therefore I say unto you, What things so ever ye desire, when ye pray, believe that ye receive *them* and ye shall have *them*.
>
> Mark 11: 22-24

The law of believing is the spiritual nature of believing. Believing produces results from the law of believing. These results are energized by spiritual power.

Believing in God is the first step to receiving from the positive side of the law of believing. This is the first great truth that must be understood if the power of God is going to effectually work in the believing heart. This is a free will choice. This choice can be likened to a railroad station that has two trains heading in opposite directions. "Doubt in his heart" is one train and "believe that ye receive" is the other. Literally, these are two trains of thought that can exist in the believing heart. Both trains are always ready to pull out of the station at any given moment in life. "Doubt in his heart" is negative believing and "believe that ye receive" is positive believing.

Even though both trains head in opposite directions, their destinations share the same name, "shall have whatsoever he saith." If we choose to believe in God and desire to receive from him, than we must stay his course to reach "shall have whatsoever he saith." This is how the power of God works in us as we believe. Positive believing brings God's power into our lives while negative believing limits and eventually negates his power. All believing, whether it is positive or negative, eventually results in energizing spiritual power in this world or in the next world to come. This is the law of believing.

### The Law of Believing

## The Free Will Choice "Rail Road Station"

### Desire

Shall Have Whatsoever He Saith…..←Believe That ye Receive

Doubt in His Heart→…..Shall Have Whatsoever He Saith

This great reality was beginning to take course and crystallize in the believing hearts of the twelve apostles. Jesus couldn't do this for them, that was their job. What he could do was teach them the spiritual nature of the law of believing and how it works in their believing hearts. The books of Mathew, Mark, Luke and John document their journey of how they built their believing hearts and learned to increase their believing. The book of Acts goes on to record how they matured to live by believing. Everyone, including those in the Bible, goes through this growth process. Learning, growing, and developing the believing heart to spiritual maturity is God's path to a successful life! It is similar to the physical growth process.

> For every one that useth milk *is* unskillful in the word of righteousness: for he is a babe.
>
> But strong meat belonged to them that are of full age, *even* those who by reason of use have their senses exercised to discern both good and evil.
>
> Hebrews 5:13, 14

The spiritual ability to discern what is good from that which is evil becomes developed as the believing heart grows from the milk of God's Word to its meat. It's a spiritual growth process the believing heart goes through as it matures. However, the ability to discern what is spiritually good from that which is spiritually evil cannot be overstated. Everyone who finished a course of believing set by God found in the Bible was strong in spiritual discernment. When a believing heart genuinely grows from the milk of God's Word to its meat, this ability will naturally develop. Furthermore, when a course of believing ends prematurely, it's because this part of the believing heart was not properly developed. This is why the personal oversight of the believing heart is the single greatest responsibility of life. Your life depends on it! The goal is to stay on the course of God's path to the finish and receive a full reward.

> Look to yourselves, that we lose not those things which we have wrought, but that we receive a full reward.
>
> 2 John 1:8

The decision to build the believing heart is the biggest decision in life. It's the biggest crossroad in life. Once a decision is made, believing begins its journey. Like the chapters in a book, believing is the pen writing the destiny of our lives. The believing heart not only determines who we will become in this world, but also in the next world to come. Matthew, chapter 7 illustrates how Jesus understood this great truth of life.

> Therefore whosoever heareth these saying of Mine, and doeth them, I will liken him unto a wise man, which built his house upon a rock;
>    And the rain descended, and the floods came, and the winds blew, and beat upon *that* house; and it fell not: for it was founded upon a rock.
>    And every one that heareth these sayings of Mine, and doeth them not, shall be likened unto a foolish man, which built his house upon the sand:
>    And the rain descended, and the floods came, and winds the winds blew, and beat upon *that* house; and it fell: and great was the fall of it.
>
> Mathew 7:24-27

Choices set the course that initiate the law of believing and determine who we will become. Who we become, reflects the outcomes produced from the law of believing. Once again, a literal example is used to illustrate the spiritual nature of believing. The houses being built not only represent the two kinds of believing hearts, but also the two courses of believing, God's path of believing and the courses of this world. There are also two kinds of builders of the believing heart. The wise man and the foolish man.

The wise man hears and builds God's Word into his believing heart. He lives by believing on God's path, developing the spiritual ability to discern, which is good and evil. When spiritual storms head in his direction, he is prepared. He has a believing heart that has unlimited strength, since it is built by the rock of God's Word. His believing is in position to receive God's way to escape the storm if needed, and always ready to take action with all things that are possible. The wise man remains standing after the storm passes. He stays on God's path throughout his lifetime finishing his course strong and becoming the wise man.

The foolish man hears but chooses not to build his believing heart on God's Word. The foolish man is comfortable with the sandy courses of believing in this world that already have been built into his believing heart. God's way is foolishness unto him. When the spiritual storms of life head in his direction, he is not prepared. He has believing that is limited to the strength of the sand. Because the truth of God's Word is missing, his believing heart falls and fails. He is unable to finish his course, and he becomes the foolish man.

> He that *hath* no rule over his own spirit *is like* a city *that is* broken down, *and* without walls.
>
> Proverbs 25:28

The strength of a believing heart is directly proportional to the Word of God within its walls. The Bible was written to build walls in the believing heart that will never fail. This is how the Word of God effectually works in us as we believe.

> For this cause also thank *we* God without ceasing, because, when ye received the word of God which ye heard of us, ye received *it* not *as* the word of men, but as it is in truth, the word of God, which effectually worketh also in you that believe.
>
> 1 Thessalonians 2:13

Collectively, this is what was happening in the believing hearts of those in Thessalonica. They changed the courses of their believing from the words of men to the words of God. Then the power of God began to work in them as they believed. God becomes the spiritual power that energizes believing in the believing heart. Below is a chart of the law of believing.

## The Law of Believing

### Desire

### Free Will Choice

*(Positive Believing)* | *Negative Believing)*

*Believe That Ye Receive* | *Doubt in His Heart*

(Positive Results) Shall Have Whatsoever He Saith (Negative Results)

Wise man | Foolish man

Since the beginning, the wise man and the foolish man have represented the two courses of believing that have been written about in history. Historically, the foolish man has gotten the best of mankind. Daily, the spiritual nature of the law of believing is at work in the believing heart determining who we will become. It's a choice and a crossroads that everyone encounters. When believing has finished its course in our lives, the wise man or the foolish man will have the final say. The wise man seeks God's ways to escape the limitations that have been put in to his believing by this world. He recognizes the goodness of God and seeks help for unbelief. By changing courses, the wise man begins to build his believing heart with the good treasures of God's Word. The power of God begins to work in him as he believes. He looks to increase his believing to the end that he lives by believing. The ability to recognize which is spiritually good and evil grows within him. He has a believing heart that is prepared for spiritual storms and his believing heart remains standing. He stays on the course and finishes strong to become the wise man. When we become the wise man that is how our destiny becomes changed! Becoming the wise man is the wise choice!

# CHAPTER 2

# THE GREATEST TREASURE

The greatest treasure that can be built into the believing heart is the love of God. This is the only core value of the believing heart that can energize the power of God. Without the love of God, the believing heart profits nothing. With the love of God, the believing heart becomes profitable and will never fail. All the great power of God found in the Bible energized into this world by those who lived by believing, will trace itself back to the love of God. Only the love of God can set a course of believing set by God. Over time it becomes the core to all decision making processes that stays the course. Only the love of God can provide the strength necessary to endure the spiritual growth process that leads us to live by believing. Only by the love of God can the power of God be consistently energized throughout the course, and enable us to finish and receive a full reward.

When the love of God energizes the power of God into this world, it will distinguish itself by producing certain qualities of life. The Bible calls them fruit of the Spirit, which means values. As the believing heart grows in the knowledge of God's Word, some of these values become learned, developed, or will naturally emanate brilliantly as a result. Galatians, chapter 5 provides a listing of some of these qualities that we can look for in ourselves, and also in others.

> But the fruit of the Spirit is love, joy, peace, long-suffering, gentleness, goodness, faith, Meekness, temperance: against such there is no law.
>
> Galatians 5:22,23

The love of God is the motive to believe in God. Motivation is the reason for the actions we take. Biblically, the believing heart is either being motivated by the love of God or hate. Eventually one will prevail over the other, energizing power from the spirit world. The Bible is filled with records of believing hearts motivated by the love of God and those by hate.

> Then went the Pharisees, and took counsel how they might entangle Him in *His* talk.
> Then one of them, *which was* a lawyer, asked *Him a question*, tempting Him, and saying,
> "Master, which *is* the great commandment in the law?"
>
> Matthew 22:15; 35,36

The Pharisees of this record looked to entangle and tempt Jesus while he was helping others learn how to live by believing. The Pharisees believing hearts demonstrated characteristics motivated by hate. Jesus demonstrated a believing heart motivated by the love of God. He understood their motives. He made the most of this situation and continues to build the believing hearts of those present.

> Jesus said unto him, "Thou shalt love the Lord
> thy God with all thy heart, and with all thy soul,
> and with all thy mind.
>
> This is the first and great commandment.
>
> And the second *is* like unto it, Thou shalt
> love thy neighbour as thyself.
>
> On these two commandments hang all the
> law and the prophets."
>
> Matthew 22:37-40

The first and greatest commandment in God's Word is to love God with all your heart, soul, and mind. This is God's mission statement for the believing heart. All decisions and actions must become subject to it. Everyone who lived by believing found in the Bible had the love of God driving their decision making process. It is the only way right spiritual decisions can made in this world. In addition, this is how the foundation of the believing heart becomes formed. To solidify the foundation, practical application of the greatest commandment must take place. This means that when the believing heart truly loves God, then practically, this same love will be demonstrated by loving your neighbor as yourself.

Not only is this truth the foundation of the believing heart, but it is also the foundation of the Word of God and the prophets. The Word of God and the prophets fall to the ground without this truth. Everyone recorded in the Bible, who lived by believing, had this foundation. This is how the power of God begins to work in us as we believe. The point in time when the love of God becomes weak in the believing heart marks the point in time when our lives begins to fall. Jesus recognized this weakness in the foundation of the believing hearts of the Pharisees. He describes the consequences that occur as a result.

> Jesus answered and said unto them, "Ye do err, not knowing the scriptures, nor the power of God.
>
> Matthew 22:29

Jesus made these comments regarding the religious leaders the people looked to for help building their believing hearts. These leaders spent their entire lives studying the Word of God and teaching the people. From the outside they looked like the greatest builders of the believing heart on the planet. On the inside, all kinds of problems existed in the foundation. Their failure to properly build the love of God in their own believing hearts caused two great errors. First, they did not properly understand the Word of God. This error invariably leads to a second error, the inability to know the power of God. To help the people further, Jesus goes into even greater detail on these great errors of the believing heart.

> Then spake Jesus to the multitude, and to His disciples,
>
> Saying, "The scribes and the Pharisees sit in Moses' seat:
>
> All therefore whatsoever they bid you observe, *that* observe and do; but do not ye after their works: for they say, and do not.
>
> For they bind heavy burdens and grievous to be borne, and lay *them* on men's shoulders; but

they *themselves* will not move them with one of their fingers.

But all their works they do for to be seen of men: they make broad their phylacteries, and enlarge the borders of their garments,

And love the uppermost rooms at feasts, and the chief seats in the synagogues,

And greetings in the markets, and to be called of men, Rabbi Rabbi.

Ye blind guides, which strain at a gnat, and swallow a camel.

Woe unto you, scribes and Pharisees, hypocrites! for ye make clean the outside of the cup and of the platter, but within they are full of extortion and excess.

*Thou* blind Pharisee, cleanse first that *which is* within the cup and platter, that the outside of them may be clean also.

Woe unto you, scribes and Pharisees, hypocrites! for ye are like unto whited sepulchres, which indeed appear beautiful outward, but are within full of dead *men's* bones, and of all uncleanness.

Matthew 23:1-7; 24-27

To say the Word of God and not do it, opens the door for these kinds of weaknesses to develop in the believing heart. This is what a believing heart looks like when the greatest commandment becomes compromised. These are characteristics of believing hearts motivated by hate. This is why Jesus called them blind guides. Jesus is the example of a believing heart built by a foundation of the great commandment. This foundation is what enabled him to understand God's Word and know the power of God.

First Corinthians, chapter 13 gives additional insight regarding the motives of the believing heart, hate and the love of God. This teaching builds upon the truths from the book of Matthew in light of the accomplishments of Jesus Christ. The key to understanding this chapter is the word charity. This word is used many times in this chapter. The proper translation of this word should be the love of God. When charity is understood to mean the love of God, then the great truth of the love of God as the foundation of the believing heart comes to light.

> Though I speak with the tongues of men and of angels, and have not charity, I am become *as* sounding brass, or a tinkling cymbal.
> And though I have *the gift* of prophecy, and understand all mysteries and all knowledge; and though I have all faith, so that I could remove mountains, and have not charity, I am nothing.
> And though I bestow all my goods to feed *the poor*, and though I give my body to be burned, and have not charity, it profiteth me nothing.
>
> 1 Corinthians 13:1-3

The first three verses of 1 Corinthians, chapter 13 restate the truth Jesus taught in the book of Matthew. A believing heart can appear beautiful on the outside, while on the inside is profiting nothing. A believing heart that profits nothing means it is not energized by the power of God. The believing heart becomes blinded, focusing on works and results over the love of God. Jesus taught,

"Cleanse first that which is within the cup and platter, that the outside of them may be clean also."

Great works of believing by themselves represent only part of the believing heart. To complete the picture, motive must be established. Motive determines the kind of spiritual power energized into this world. Profitable believing energizes the power of God into this world. Unprofitable believing energizes the power of the devil into this world. All energized believing ends in judgment, which is either revealed in this world or the next world to come. In this world, not all energized believing is revealed. In the next world to come, all energized believing is revealed and nothing can be hidden. Judgment is the final outcome from the law of believing by energized believing.

> Some men's sins are open beforehand, going before to judgment; and some *men* they follow after.
>
> Likewise also the good works *of some* are manifest beforehand; and they that are otherwise cannot be hid.
>
> 1 Timothy 5:24,25

To the outside world, a believing heart can appear as a great believing heart that removes mountains. It can appear as the most generous and giving heart on the planet. However, on the inside, something is wrong. Hate has prevailed over the love of God and profits nothing.

The rest of 1 Corinthians, chapter 13 describes what would be found when a profitable believing heart is opened and examined. All its moving parts, what it will do and what it will not do, become revealed. Bringing to light a complete picture of a mature believing heart founded upon the love of God. (Biblically charity in this usage means the love of God and faith means believing)

> Charity suffereth long, *and* is kind; charity envieth not; charity vaunted not itself, is not puffed up,
>
> Doth not behave itself unseemly, seeketh not her own, is not easily provoked, thinketh no evil;
>
> Rejoiceth not in iniquity, but rejoiceth in the truth;
>
> Beareth all things, believeth all things, hopeth all things, endureth all things.
>
> Charity never faileth: but whether *there be* prophecies, they shall fail; whether *there be* tongues, they shall cease; whether *there* be knowledge, it shall vanish away.
>
> For we know in part and we prophesy in part.
>
> But when that which is perfect is come, then that which is in part shall be done away.
>
> When I was a child, I spake as a child: I understood as a child, I thought as a child: but when I became a man, I put away childish things.
>
> For now we see through a glass, darkly; but then face to face: now I know in part; but then shall I know even as also I am known.
>
> And now abideth faith, hope, charity, these three; but the greatest of these *is* charity.
>
> 1 Corinthians 13:4-13

Building a sound and solid foundation on the love of God in the believing heart is the greatest work we can do in our lives. It's the one thing guaranteed by God to never fail. Could God give any greater emphasis to the importance of the solid foundation of the love of God in the believing heart? The love of God is a greater truth than believing and hope. It's the greatest truth in the Bible and that's why it's called the greatest commandment. Many benefits from God will be realized in our lives, as the love of God in the believing heart is maintained and protected. 1 John, chapter 4 instructs us of these benefits.

> There is no fear in love; but perfect love casteth out fear: because fear hath torment. He that feareth is not made perfect in love.
>
> 1 John 4:18

At the same time that the love of God is being properly built into the believing heart, fear is being cast out. The only antidote that cures fear is the love of God. Fear cannot exist with the love of God, just as light cannot exist with darkness. They are mutually exclusive. Fear and torment are spiritual storms upon the love of God in the believing heart. Great understanding of the love of God is the rock in the believing heart that weathers these storms.

Galatians, chapter 5 builds more understanding of the spiritual relationship that exists between the love of God and the law of believing. We learn the specific details of how the power of God works in us, as we believe.

> For in Jesus Christ neither circumcision availeth anything, nor uncircumcision; but faith [biblically means believing] which worketh[means energize] by love.
>
> Galatians 5:6

The believing heart is first spiritual, thus governed by spiritual law. Works of the flesh are secondary. When the love of God motivates the believing heart, the result will be energized power of God brought into this world. This is the meaning of, "Faith which worketh by love." The love of God drives the actions of the believing heart that produces results from the law of believing on the positive side. The power of God only becomes energized by the love of God. This is how a course of believing set by God begins and is maintained.

## The Law of Believing
### Free Will Choice

| (Positive Believing) | | (Negative Believing) |
|---|---|---|
| *Love of God* | | *Hate* |
| *Believing Energized by Love of God* | | *Fear Energized by Hate* |
| Power of God | | Power of The Devil |
| Enters This World | | Enters This World |

The greatest treasure that can be built into the believing heart is the love of God. Only by its strength (love, joy, peace, longsuffering, gentleness, goodness, faith, meekness, temperance) can a course of believing set by God be finished to receive a full reward. Building and protecting this foundation is the most important work in life over everything else. The first and greatest commandment teaches us how to build the love of God into our believing hearts, "Thou shalt love the Lord thy God with all thy heart, and with all thy soul, and with all thy mind." The second greatest commandment teaches how to practically apply this in life, "Thou shalt love thy neighbor as thyself." The love of God is a motive of the believing heart. Only two motives can energize believing and bring spiritual power into this world. Love or hate. The further the believing heart drifts from the love of God, as its motive, the further the believing heart is capable of understanding the Word of God and the power of God. Building the love of God into the believing heart is first an inside job. Jesus taught, "Cleanse first that which is within the cup and platter, that the outside of them may be clean also." Love of works without the love of God first, are characteristic of hate motivating the believing heart. First Corinthians, chapter 13 is a study of these two motives and the profit they bring to our lives. The believing heart motivated by hate profits nothing and fails. It can appear beautiful on the outside having believing to remove mountains, but on the inside is all spiritual uncleanness. In contrast, the believing heart, motivated by the love of God, is profitable and never fails. All energized believing ends in judgment, which may be seen in this world. In the next world to come, all energized believing is revealed. Only the love of God can energize the power of God. Living by believing is when the love of God drives the actions that produce results from the law of believing on the positive side. Only the love of God, within a believing heart that energizes the power of God, can cast out fear. This is why the love of God is the greatest truth, greater than believing and hope. The love of God is the greatest treasure of the good treasures of the Word of God found in the believing heart!

# CHAPTER 3

# THE MASTER BELIEVING HEART

G reat believing is the power of God working mightily in us, as we believe. It's believing, but at the masters level. There will be points during a course of believing set by God that the believing heart will be challenged to rise to this level. This is why God calls all believing hearts to master believing. When mastery is fully developed, the fundamentals of believing are second nature, not only to meet difficult spiritual challenges, but to win them. The Bible is filled with examples of those who had master believing hearts. Notably they include, Jesus Christ, the Roman centurion from Capernaum, and Abraham. The first fundamental of great believing is to believe in God and that he rewards those that diligently seek him.

> But without faith *it is* impossible to please *Him*: for he that cometh to God must believe that He is, and *that* He is a rewarder of them that diligently seek Him.
>
> Hebrews 11:6

Mastery of believing begins by building the fundamentals. Living by believing which is a daily repetition of the fundamentals, prepares the believing heart for even greater believing. Moderation in all things is how the believing heart stays balanced.

> Let your moderation be known unto all men. The LORD *is* at hand.
>
> Philippians 4:5

All believing hearts start out walking and then learn to run. All those who live by believing follow this course.

> I will run the way of Thy commandments, When Thou shalt enlarge my heart.
>
> Psalms 119:32

The power of God working mightily in us increases as the capacity of the believing heart enlarges. This is what increasing believing is all about. God desires all those who will live by believing to become stronger in the power of his might.

> Finally, my brethren, be strong in the LORD, and in the power of His might.
>
> Ephesians 6:10

Great believing is about becoming spiritually minded and sensitive to the spiritual power being brought into this world by your own believing heart and that of others. It's about paying attention to the details in God's Word, in life, and if possible leaving no stone unturned spiritually, mentally, and physically, all the time. Everything is on the spiritual radar all the time. Little things and big things. Great believing is about being in control of things we can control, like the physical things of life, so to be entrusted with the spiritual things of God.

> For to be carnally minded *is* death; but to be spiritually minded *is* life and peace.
>
> Romans 8:6

Great believing is about the peace of God ruling in our believing hearts. Biblically, peace means undisturbed, focused believing. Peace rules in the believing heart by separating what is spiritually good from what is evil. Evil has no place in the peaceful believing heart. However, peace is maintained by offensive and defensive spiritual strategies against evil.

> For your obedience is come abroad unto all *men*. I am glad therefore on your behalf: but yet I would have you wise unto that which is good, and simple concerning evil.
>
> And the God of peace shall bruise Satan under your feet shortly. The grace of our LORD Jesus Christ *be* with you. Amen.
>
> Romans 16:19,20

Great believing delivers the blow to Satan, instead of receiving the blow from Satan! Great believing delivers aggression, instead of receiving aggression! Great believing is being the hunter, instead of being the hunted! (Biblically faith in this usage means believing).

> Holding faith, and a good conscience; which some having put away, concerning faith have made shipwreck:
> Of whom is Hymenaeus and Alexander; whom I have delivered unto Satan, that they may learn not to blaspheme.
>
> I Timothy 1:19,20

Great believing is being on your toes spiritually, instead of being on your heels. It's an attitude that is valiant for truth, always moving forward, and increasing believing, instead of back peddling in fear. It's not about being perfect, but being faithful, and realizing that life is spiritual and meant to be lived by believing.

> I will not be afraid of ten thousands of people, that have set *themselves* against me round about.
> Arise, O LORD; save me, O my God: For Thou hast smitten all mine enemies *upon* the cheek bone; Thou hast broken the teeth of the ungodly.
> Salvation *belonged* unto the LORD: Thy blessing *is* upon Thy People. Selah. [Biblically, Selah means deeply consider this]
>
> Psalms 3:6-8

Great believing never quits, and it always strives to win. It's a deep and unmovable understanding that good will always triumph over evil, no matter what circumstance. It's a noble way of life, doing good and helping others who are oppressed by the devil.

> How God anointed Jesus of Nazareth with the Holy Ghost and with power; Who went about doing good, and healing all that were oppressed of the devil; for God was with Him.
>
> Acts 10:38

Satan will disrupt all courses of believing set by God. God desires that all believing hearts learn to run and obtain his promises to overcome evil. A believing heart that has great strength is exemplified by great believing.

> Know ye not that they which run in a race run all, but one receiveth the prize? So run that ye may obtain.
>
> And every man that striveth for the mastery is temperate in all things.
>
> Now *they* do *it* to obtain a corruptible crown: but *we* an incorruptible.
>
> *I* therefore so run, not as uncertainly; so fight [Biblically run and fight mean the master level of believing, great believing] I, not as one that beateth the air:
>
> But I keep under my body, and bring *it* into subjection: lest that by any means, when I have preached to others, I myself should be a castaway.
>
> 1 Corinthians 9:24-27

This section of 1 Corinthians, chapter 9 is talking about great believing. A literal athletic example is used to teach the spiritual lessons of great believing. God's desire for the believing heart is winning. This means applying similar concepts of discipline that elite athletes live by. To compete at the highest levels requires being mentally and physically fit, including self-control. Moses competed at these levels, and when he finished his course, his physical body remained strong.

> And Moses *was* an hundred and twenty years old when he died: his eye was not dim, nor his natural force abated.
>
> Deuteronomy 34:7

All believing hearts striving for mastery of believing must become self-controlled in all things, just as elite athletes must do to stay competitive. 1 Corinthians, chapter 9: 27 states that anything less is to become a castaway.

Instead of becoming a master runner or boxer, God's desire is that the believing heart strives to master believing. A master believing heart that runs with certainty and outdistances evil, will win the prize. A master believing heart does not beat the air, but hits the spiritual enemies. Instead of corruptible crowns, the master believing heart is obtaining incorruptible spiritual crowns. A master believing heart can only produce great believing according to the rules of the spiritual competition. The rule book of the spiritual competition is the Bible.

The most difficult and challenging course of believing was completed by Jesus Christ. This course required following every detail of truth found in the Bible to complete God's plan of redemption while destroying the works of the devil, including eternal death. By finishing this course, unconditional eternal life became available unto all those who following after, would receive by believing. No man has ever borne more responsibility to God in their course of believing. No man has ever knowingly had so much at stake and on the line. This is why Jesus Christ is the greatest example of great believing. His course required nothing less than an enlarged believing heart capable of thwarting every attack brought on by the devil. Fortunately for mankind, Jesus Christ did finish this course and earned for himself the greatest honor bestowed by God recorded in the Bible and throughout all history.

> Wherefore God also hath highly exalted Him, and give Him a name which is above every name:
> That at the name of Jesus every knee should bow, of *things* in heaven, and *things* in earth, and *things* under the earth;
> And *that* every tongue should confess that Jesus Christ *is* LORD, to the glory of God the Father.
>
> Philippians 2:9-11

The Bible is the record of how Jesus Christ finished the greatest course of believing ever lived, bringing to light the truths of great believing.

> Hereby perceive we the love *of God*, because *he* laid down His life for us: and *we* ought to lay down *our* lives for the brethren.
> But whoso hath this world's good, and seeth his brother have need, and shutteth up his bowels *of compassion* from him, how dwelleth the love of God in him?

> My little children, let us not love in word nei-
> ther in tongue; but in deed and in truth.

> 1 John 3:16-18

Laying down one's life for others is the greatest level of commitment that can be reached in the believing heart. Jesus had this level of commitment in his love for God. Commitment is a core value of the believing heart that solidifies the greatest core value—the love of God. The believing heart can never reach its potential without great commitment. When great commitment exists, the eyes of the believing heart become open, seeing the needs of others and feeling compassion. The compassionate love of God gives in service and of this world's goods to help others. The love of God in the believing heart is perceived in deed and in truth.

The Bible is filled with examples of great believing. Each has its own unique lessons. Just as no two people are exactly alike, neither are two believing hearts. They vary. However, great believing unites them all. Luke, chapter 7 is a record of great believing.

> Now when He had ended all His saying in the audi-
> ence of the people, He entered into Capernaum.
>
> And a certain centurion's servant, who was dear unto him, was sick, and ready to die.
>
> And when he heard of Jesus, he sent unto Him the elders of the Jews, beseeching Him that He would come and heal his servant.
>
> And when they came to Jesus, they besought Him instantly, saying, that he was worthy for whom He should do this:

> "For he loveth our nation, and *he* hath built
> us a synagogue."
>
> Luke 7:1-5

This record begins with a need for healing, as a certain Roman centurion's servant lay sick and ready to die. The Roman centurion counted his dying servant dear, meaning that he was esteemed and honored. Roman centurions were the equivalent to a captain in the Roman army. Often, these men rose from the ranks to centurion on account of bravery and military efficiency. In every military discipline, the drill, the march, or in battle, the centurion was proven. It was the Roman centurion who set the standards of excellence for other soldiers to follow.

This specific Roman centurion from Luke, chapter 7 was stationed in Capernaum. This is where his course of believing set by God began and set him apart in many ways. He learned to love the nation of Israel in spite of his position of leadership and all other conflicting cultural differences. He built for those who lived by believing, a new synagogue. The synagogue was the place where the people learned God's Word and how to live by believing. He also was counted worthy by the Judean elders for Jesus to come and heal his servant. This record is a demonstration of how a committed believing heart increases in believing, from walk to run, from the milk of God's Word to its meat. It grows from working to build the believing heart, to developing an enlarged master believing heart capable of great believing. Jesus recognized the great believing showed by the Roman centurion's enlarged believing heart, and took action.

> Then Jesus went with them. And when He was now not far from the house, the centurion sent friends to Him, saying unto Him, "Lord, trouble not Thyself: for I am not worthy that Thou shouldest enter under my roof:
>
> Wherefore neither thought I myself worthy to come unto Thee: but say in a word, and my servant shall be healed.
>
> For *I* also am a man set under authority, having under me soldiers, and I say unto one, 'Go,' and he goeth; and to another, 'Come,' and he cometh; and to my servant, 'Do this,' and he doeth *it*."
>
> When Jesus heard these things, He marveled at him, and turned Him about, and said unto the people that followed Him, "I say unto you, I have not found so great faith, no, not in Israel."
>
> And they that were sent, returning to the house, found the servant whole that had been sick.
>
> Luke 7:6-10

No greater honor could have been given by Jesus to the Roman centurion than, "I say unto you, I have not found so great faith, no, not in Israel." The Roman centurion didn't need Jesus to come over and heal his servant. All he needed from Jesus was to hear that his servant would be healed. That was it! He understood the finer details of great believing and its relationship to obedience. His life and all those under his command, which included his honored servant depended on it. This was the quality that inspired Jesus to categorize the Roman centurion's believing, as great believing!

Abraham is another inspiring example of great believing. His course included keeping the genealogical Christ-line going during prolonged intense attacks brought on by Satan. He, along with his wife Sarah, understood what was at stake and together they finished this tremendously difficult course, earning for Abraham the great honor being called, "the father of all them that believe", "father of many nations", and "friend of God." Romans, chapter 4 talks about the qualities of his great believing heart.

> (As it is written, "I have made thee a father of many nations") before Him Whom he believed, *even* God, Who quickened the dead, and calleth those things which be not, as though they were.
>
> Who against hope believed in hope, that he might become the father of many nations, according to that which was spoken, "so shall thy seed be."
>
> And being not weak in weak faith, he considered not his own body now dead, when he was about an hundred years old, neither yet the deadness of Sarah's womb:
>
> He staggered not at the promise of God through unbelief: but was strong in faith, giving glory to God;
>
> And being fully persuaded that, what He had promised, He was able also to perform.
>
> Romans 4:17-21

Abraham understood life was spiritual and that he and his wife Sarah needed to master believing and, when necessary, have great believing if they were to inherit the promises of God. They chose to master believing. Their hearts became enlarged and capable of great believing. Abraham had great commitment in his love for God and obeyed. He refused to allow his believing heart to stagger in unbelief. Instead, he and Sarah became fully persuaded that what God had promised, He was also able to perform. Even when their bodies appeared dead, Sarah conceived and bore Isaac, continuing the Christ-line.

All believing hearts will be challenged by Satan, but the master believing heart always prevails! Great believing will be necessary at times in order to finish the course of believing set by God. Great believing is a special level of believing, a masters level. All believing hearts start out walking and enlarge as they learn to run. Great believing is about being spiritually minded all the time. It's about being the hunter instead of the hunted. It's a course that learns self-control in all things, and one that learns how to run with focus and strike the enemy according to God's Word. Jesus Christ finished the greatest course of believing that was ever set by God. The commitment level of his love for God was exemplified when he laid down his life, so that all those who followed after, would believe. Jesus earned for himself the greatest honors bestowed by God that can be found in the Bible. The Roman centurion followed his course of believing set by God in spite of many cultural contradictions. His obedience and great believing healed his servant and inspired

Jesus to say, "I say unto you, I have not found so great faith, no, not in Israel." Abraham and his wife Sarah staggered not at the promises of God but finished a very difficult course, giving glory to God. Abraham earned great honor from God becoming, "the father of all them that believe", "the father of many nations" and "friend of God." All the heroes that had great believing found in the Bible are examples to the believing heart, sending a message to us all. Rise up and begin walking. Learn to run and enlarge, becoming capable of great believing. Finish the course set for you by God and obtain a full reward. These are the underlying truths of the master believing heart.

# CHAPTER 4

# THE POWER OF GOD

A believing heart stands by the power of God. It's how a course of believing is finished to receive its full reward. The Bible is where this wisdom can be found.

> That your faith should not stand in the wisdom of men, but in the power of God.
>
> 1 Corinthians 2:5

The wisdom of the power of God is one of the greatest treasures found in the Bible. This is the wisdom that sustains the course of believing set by God. It's the fundamental principle to live by daily.

> Brethren, I count not myself to have apprehended: but this one thing I do, forgetting those things which are behind, and reaching forth unto those things which are before,
> I press toward the mark for the prize of the high calling of God in Christ Jesus.
>
> Philippians 3:13,14

These verses from Philippians chapter 3 reveal two important keys regarding a consistent energized believing heart. This is what pressing toward the mark or toward the finish is all about. The first key is developing daily habits of reaching forward. Reaching forward is the believing action of the heart known as works. Good works of believing are works energized by the power of God. These are the hands and arms of the believing heart in motion. These works allow God to be part of our lives. It's how to stay the course of believing set by God on a daily basis. Sometimes it's hard work, but it's always a worthwhile work. Most of the time it's a joyful work when consistently applied. Benefits include rewards from God now and throughout all eternity. It's the greatest way to go through this life. Nothing is better. Good works and believing go together. Believing alone without works is dead.

> Even so faith, if it hath not works, is dead, being alone.
> Yea, a man may say, "*Thou* hast faith, and *I* have works: shew me thy faith without thy works, and *I* will shew thee my faith by my works."
>
> James 2:17,18

The other great spiritual truth from Philippians, chapter 3 is the willingness to forget the sins of the past and the sins that come up that have already been forgiven while on a course of believing set by God. To forgive is to forget. To forget is to reach forth. The past cannot be changed, but the future can be. Past experiences can be healed, but only by moving forward and reaching forth with energized works of believing. This involves giving;

the giving of ourselves and the giving of our plurality to help others.

The law of giving is seen throughout The Bible. When we give with the love of God, we will receive back at a minimum what we need. Good works of believing takes the focus off of our own lives, while helping others get their need met. This is why the ability to forget the sins of the past is critical for the power of God to consistently energize the believing heart. Satan knows this truth and will do everything possible to stop the power of God from energizing. Failing to forget sins allows Satan to gain a foothold in the believing heart that impedes the power of God. This is how the believing heart can become its own worst enemy. Satan will also work through people knowledgeable of past sins. Guarding the believing heart is how to keep Satan from disrupting the course of believing that has been set by God.

> Keep[biblically, means to guard] thy heart with all diligence; For out of it *are* the issues of life.
>
> Proverbs 4:23

Every day is a new opportunity for the power of God to energize. Not only does this include getting your needs met, but also the needs of others. These truths can be found in those that press towards the mark, and finish.

> Look not every man on his own things, but every man also on the things of others.
>
> Philippians 2:4

One of the great believing hearts that sought the wisdom of the power of God belonged to Solomon. His books and life as king of Israel, record how God mightily energized his believing heart. 2 Chronicles, chapter 1 takes up just before Solomon was to become king of Israel. Many of the truths about the power of God come to light through his course.

> And Solomon went up thither to the brazen altar before the LORD, which *was* at the tabernacle of the congregation, and offered a thousand burnt offerings upon it.
> In that night did God appear unto Solomon, and said unto him, "Ask what I shall give thee."
>
> 2 Chronicles 1:6,7

These works of energized believing reflect the great treasures of the love of God and the wisdom of the power of God that Solomon had built into his believing heart. Great treasure leads to great receiving from God. In this record, God asked Solomon, "Ask what I shall give thee." On the surface, this seems too good to be true. From the inside of Solomon's believing heart, an entirely different perspective existed. A spiritual perspective that revealed the great treasures of the wisdom of the power of God that led to great reward. These treasures are found in Solomon's book of Proverbs.

> My Son, if thou wilt receive my words, And hide my commandments with thee;
> So that thou incline thine ear unto wisdom, *and* apply thine heart to understanding;

> Yea, if thou criest after knowledge, *And* liftest up thy voice for understanding;
>
> If thou seekest her as silver, And searchest for her as *for* hid treasurers;
>
> *Then* shalt thou understand the fear of the LORD, and find the knowledge of God.

Proverbs 2:1-5

These were the kind of treasures inside Solomon's believing heart when God asked him, "Ask what I shall give thee." When these treasures of the wisdom of the power of God are built into the believing heart, then the power of God will be energized. God cannot be fooled. This is the course of believing set by God that energizes the power of God.

> And Solomon said unto God, "*Thou* hast shewed great mercy unto David my father, and hast made me to reign in his stead.
>
> Now, O LORD God, let Thy promise unto David my father be established: for *Thou* hast made me king over a People like the dust of the earth in multitude.
>
> Give me now wisdom and knowledge that I may go out and come in before this People: for who can judge this Thy People, *that is so* great?"
>
> And God said to Solomon, "Because this was in thine heart, and thou hast not asked riches, wealth, or honour, nor the life of thine enemies, neither yet hast asked long life; but hast asked wisdom and knowledge for thyself, that thou

mayest judge My People, over whom I have
made thee king:

Wisdom and knowledge *is* granted unto
thee; and I will give thee riches, and wealth, and
honour, such as none of the kings have had that
*have been* before thee, neither shall there any
after thee have the like."

2 Chronicles 1:8-12

God's interests begin on the inside of the believing
heart, what is inside and what is not. The energized
power of God is always at stake. Solomon didn't build
his believing heart with treasures of riches, wealth, and
honor. Nor was it filled with treasures against his enemies
or his own long life. This is the limited wisdom of men.
His treasure was the love of God and the wisdom of the
power of God. These treasures produced thoughts about
what God had done for his father, about the needs of
the people, and increasing his own believing so he could
meet those needs as a king. This is one of the Bible's
greatest examples of a believing heart desiring to reach
forth with energized good works of believing.

When God said, "Ask what I shall give thee",
Solomon had already prepared his heart with the wisdom
of the power of God. His focus was on the things before
him as king. He knew he needed more of the power
of God energizing his believing heart to carry out the
great responsibilities as king of Israel. To receive more
power from God, He asked for God's wisdom and God's
knowledge. This is how to receive the power of God.
This is the kind of believing heart that pleases God and
gets rewarded. Solomon not only received God's wisdom

and knowledge; but also riches, wealth, and honor such as none of the kings before or after him. This was how Solomon's great-believing heart enabled God to do exceedingly abundantly above all he could ask or think. This is how great love of God and the wisdom of the power of God energizes great believing.

> For the LORD giveth wisdom: out of his mouth *cometh* knowledge and understanding.
>
> Proverbs 2:6

The believing heart needs the great treasurers of God's wisdom, knowledge, and understanding built within. Together they're the wisdom of the power of God. The believing heart is meant to be filled with them, and that's when it will function the best. This is how the power of God becomes energized. When the power of God is energized, it's the law of believing on the positive side in action.

## The Law of Believing (The Positive Side)

### *Motivation: Love of God*

### Gods Knowledge

### *Gods Wisdom*

### The Power of God: God's Understanding

Wisdom, knowledge, and understanding are found together throughout the Bible. The more that can be learned about these great treasures, the more the power of God can be realized by believing. Proverbs chapter 24 takes an even deeper look into this truth.

> Through wisdom is a house built; and by under-
> standing, it is established
>   and by knowledge shall the chambers be
> filled with all precious and pleasant riches.
>
> Proverbs 24:3,4

Many times in the Bible, the believing heart is represented as a literal house to teach a great spiritual truth.
In this example; wisdom, understanding, and knowledge
represent the course a believing heart goes through as
it is built by God's Word. It's compared to the same
process a house goes through as it becomes established.
First, it must become built, then furnished, and finally,
over time established.

Proverbs 24 begins by building the house by wisdom.
First, the foundation is laid by the great commandment
of the love of God. Growing from the milk of God's
Word to its meat is similar to the building process of a
house. Starting from the foundation (milk) to its roof
(meat). Wisdom means application of the knowledge of
God's Word. Every time the Word of God is applied,
it becomes stronger. It remains strong by continuing to
apply God's Word, staying its course of believing, and
reaching forth with energized works of believing. Just
as a literal house is built and framed, the believing heart
becomes built and framed by God's Word as it learns
and applies it. Once built it will need to become established and furnished.

If a believing heart is going stand on God's Word
for a lifetime, it must become established. The spiritually
established believing heart is similar to an established

house, one that over time has withstood everything that has tried to tear it down. Similarly, the believing heart becomes established by spiritual understanding. Spiritual understanding means experience. The experienced believing heart is a master believing heart. Experience is developed by competing in the spiritual competition between good and evil. Only a master believing heart can run the spiritual course set by God with certainty and hit enemy targets. To become established, the master believing heart will have been weathered by many great spiritual storms and remains standing. The established house referred to in Proverbs, chapter 24 is a literal example of what a master believing heart looks like.

Like all homes become furnished, all believing hearts become furnished with something. The believing heart filled with God's knowledge, is like precious and pleasant riches that fill the rooms of a well decorated house. This is what the believing heart should look like from the inside out. This is what all established believing hearts found in the Bible looks like from the inside out.

Knowledge, wisdom and understanding complete the law of believing on the positive side. The goal of believing is to reach spiritual understanding in the believing heart. In the New Testament one of the Greek words used to translate understanding is the Greek word *sunesis*. From 2 Timothy chapter 2, the meaning of sunesis uncovers more depth of the believing heart.

> Consider what I say; and the LORD give thee understanding in all things.
>
> 2 Timothy 2:7

*Sunesis* is the point where two rivers meet and become one. The point of becoming one is an understanding. Similarly, when the rivers of God's knowledge and wisdom meet and become one, spiritual understanding takes place in the believing heart. This new river formed in the believing heart is spiritual understanding, also known as the wisdom of the power of God. This is the point when the power of God becomes energized, and rewards for believing are received. It is also the point when a new course of believing is set by God for the new believer. This is what takes place in the believing heart that once was blind but now can see. For those who live by believing, this is how to stay the course and win rewards. These rewards of the power of God are not limited to great signs, miracles, and wonders. They also include great treasures of spiritual understanding. Spiritual understanding is the ultimate treasure. It's how the believing heart becomes established, to becoming the wise man, able to spiritually discern good and evil.

> But strong meat belonged to them that are of full age, *even* those who by reason of use have their senses exercised to discern good and evil.
>
> Hebrews 5:14

This spiritual growth process enables God to give spiritual understanding in all things. Most importantly, developing the ability to separate and discern which is of God, and which is of the devil. This is a spiritual growth process, whereby over time, all five senses of the believing heart become developed. The eyes, ears, nose, taste, and touch become adept at discerning motives, actions, and which spiritual power is at work energizing the law of believing. Colossians, chapter 1 emphasizes this great truth.

> For this cause *we* also, since the day we heard *it*, do not cease to pray for you, and to desire that ye might be filled with the knowledge of His will in all wisdom and spiritual understanding;
>
> That ye might walk[means to believe] worthy of the LORD unto all pleasing, being fruitful in every good work, and increasing in the knowledge of God;
>
> Colossians 1:9,10

God's desire is for spiritual understanding to always take place in the believing heart. Increasing in God's knowledge is the first step. This is how the believing heart becomes and stays filled with knowledge of his will. Knowledge alone is not enough. It must be applied (God's wisdom). Once God's knowledge has been applied, spiritual understanding can be received and the power of God will manifest itself in every good work of believing. This is the deeper truth regarding believing that is pleasing to God. Ephesians, chapter 1 establishes the believing heart with more of this great truth.

> That the God of our LORD Jesus Christ, the Father of glory, may give unto you the spirit of wisdom and revelation in the knowledge of Him:
>
> The eyes of your understanding being enlightened, that ye may know what is the hope of His calling, and what the riches of the glory of His inheritance in the saints,[means those who have received holy spirit and live by believing]

> And what *is* the exceeding greatness of His power to us-ward who believe, according to the working of His mighty power,
>
> Which he wrought in Christ, when He raised Him from the dead, and set *Him* at His own right hand in heavenly *places*,
>
> Far above all principality, and power, and might, and dominion, and every name that is named, not only in this world, but also in that which is to come:
>
> And hath put all *things* under His feet, and gave Him *to be* the Head over all *things* to the church.
>
> Which is His body, the fulness of Him That filleth all in all.
>
> Ephesians 1:17-23

The spiritual understanding, which takes place in the believing heart regarding the accomplishments of Jesus Christ, is one of the great treasures the believing heart can receive from God. When this occurs for the first time, the power of God becomes energized, and the gift of the holy spirit is received. Then the believing heart is spiritually equipped to receive the spirit of wisdom and revelation knowledge. This is how the eyes of the believing heart become enlightened to understand the hope of his calling, the riches of the inheritance of the saints, and the exceeding greatness of his power to those who believe. This spiritual understanding is the wisdom of the power of God and how the just live by believing.

> For I am not ashamed of the gospel of Christ: for it is the power of God unto salvation to every one that believeth; to the Jew first, and also the Greek.

> For therein is the righteousness of God revealed from faith to faith: as it is written "The just shall live by faith."
>
> Romans 1:16,17

A believing heart stands by the power of God. The wisdom of the power of God is how the power of God energizes in the believing heart. To live by believing, the power of God must consistently energize the believing heart. To stay consistently energized, two great spiritual truths must be applied on a daily basis. First, the arms of the believing heart must reach forward daily to carry out energized good works of believing. Secondly, the believing heart must learn how to forget sins of the past that already have been forgiven. Satan knows our sins and will tirelessly work to bring them up. Reaching out and forgetting is how to live daily by believing. One of the greatest persons ever to live by believing was Solomon. Solomon searched for and found the wisdom of the power of God. He founded his believing heart with the love of God and sought to enlarge it with great believing. This allowed God to ask Solomon what he wanted from Him. Solomon understood his greatest need and asked for more of God's knowledge, and God's wisdom. What Solomon was asking for was the wisdom of the power of God. Because this filled his believing heart, God was able to energize his believing heart as king of Israel like no other king before or after him. Not only did God give Solomon what he asked for, he also gave him things he didn't ask for. Solomon developed great spiritual understanding as a result of the power of God energizing his believing heart. He taught how the law of believing on the positive side builds the believing heart. Specifically, he taught how the believing heart is built by God's wisdom, filled with God's knowledge, and becomes established by God's spiritual understanding.

Spiritual understanding is formed within the believing heart when the rivers of God's knowledge and wisdom become one, energizing the power of God. Only by the power of God energizing, can the wisdom of the power of God be received. This is how the power of God not only will meet our needs, but also the needs of others. This is how the eyes of the spiritual heart become enlightened regarding Jesus Christ, the hope of his calling, the riches of his inheritance in the saints, and the exceeding greatness of His power as we believe. It is how all of the spiritual senses of the believing heart become developed, discerning that which is of God and that which is of the devil. God's desire is that the power of God consistently energize the believing heart, being fruitful in every daily good work. This is the wisdom of the power of God.

# CHAPTER 5

# GOD'S GRACE AND MERCY

Everything benefits from God's grace and mercy. Grace means unmerited divine favor. It can't be earned; it's a gift of God. Mercy means withholding of the ultimate negative outcome of the law of believing, death. Together, they are the last line of defense against the devil. It's the power of God that keeps the devil from prematurely ending a course of believing. God's grace and mercy are the borderline between life and death. It's a point of unbelief in the believing heart where the walls of the love of God in the believing heart become weakened by hate, but hate is unable to prevail. The love of God holds firm, keeping Satan from killing. However, hate energizes the power of the devil, resulting in the law of believing from the negative side to produce negative results. God's grace and mercy is the middle section of the law of believing, where both positive and negative believing are energized. This is indicative of a weak or immature believing heart.

The Law of Believing (The Middle Section)

Motivation

Love of God | Love God | Hate

| *Positive Side* | *God's Grace and Mercy* | *Negative Side* |
|---|---|---|
| *Positive Believing* | *Positive/Negative* | *Negative Believing* |
| Positive Outcomes | Pos/Neg Outcomes | Negative Outcomes |

Who receives God's grace and mercy and who does not is always dependant on what's in the believing heart at that moment. Nothing happens by luck or chance. Things happen when spiritual power becomes energized and enters this world. All believing hearts are subject to the spirit world, its laws, and the two great spiritual powers, God and the devil.

For there is no respect of persons with God.

Romans 2:11

God is the greatest spiritual power in the spirit world. He does not play favorites. God's desire is that believing hearts be filled with spiritual understanding and receive the reward of believing. His Word reveals the great knowledge of the spirit world, its past and its future. God has put limits, set boundaries, and allowed himself to go above and beyond what he has promised in his Word. He knows the future, the decisions that will be made, and the course a believing heart will take.

> The heart *is* deceitful above all *things*, and
> desperately wicked: who can know it?
>
> *I* the LORD search the heart, I try the reins[means
> thoughts], even to give every man according to his
> ways, *and* according to the fruit[means the out-
> comes of the law of believing] of his doings.
>
> Jeremiah 17:9,10

God is the only spiritual power that knows what we
are thinking. He created the law of believing to give
every man the same opportunities. When believing
energizes spiritual power, fruit is produced. All fruit is an
outcome of the law of believing. These outcomes become
evidenced in this world or in the next world to come.
The two ruling spiritual powers are the source of all fruit.
One power is God and the other is the devil. These two
spiritual powers have been at war long before Adam and
Eve. However, since Adam and Eve, the believing heart
has been the focus of this war. Only by mastering believing can the ability to separate the two powers be developed. The Bible distinguishes their differences.

> This then is the message which we have heard of
> him, and declare unto you, that God is light, and
> in him is no darkness at all.
>
> 1 John 1:5

God is light, and it's impossible for him to produce
dark fruit. Darkness does not exist in God. The devil is
total darkness and is the source of all dark fruit.

> To open their eyes, *and* to turn *them* from dark-
> ness to light, and *from* the power of Satan unto
> God, that they may receive forgiveness of sins,
> and inheritance among them which are sancti-
> fied by faith that is in me.
>
> Acts 26:18

The power of darkness belongs to Satan and the
power of light belongs to God. James, chapter 1 separates
the fruit produced by these two great spiritual powers.

> Every good gift[means the positive outcomes
> of the law of believing] and every perfect gift is
> from above, and cometh down From the Father
> of lights, with whom is no variableness, neither
> shadow of turning.
>
> James 1:17

God's gifts or fruit, have no change in them or shadow
of turning. These characteristics are found in the devil's
fruit. All fruit produced by the power of the devil will
eventually go bad, in this world or will be exposed in the
next world to come. Sometimes his fruit is very apparent
to the spiritual eye, and sometimes only possible to be seen
by God's revelation. The devil's power of darkness works
by unbelief, deception, and disguising his fruit. He deceives
the whole world by his courses of spiritual blindness.

> For such *are* false apostles, deceitful workers, trans-
> forming themselves into the apostles of Christ.
> And no marvel; for Satan himself is trans-
> formed into an angel of light.

> Therefore *it is* no great thing if his ministers
> also be transformed as the ministers of righteous-
> ness; whose end shall be according to their works.
>
> 2 Corinthians 11:13-15

When a course of believing is set by God, then His power begins to work in us to separate the two great spiritual powers at work in this world. That is the only way a believing heart can escape a course of spiritual blindness set by Satan. Unbelief, which is fear, is spiritual blindness caused by the power of darkness. Spiritual understanding is the only cure and once it is built into the believing heart energizes the power of light. Then the eyes of the believing heart can be opened, turning it from the power of Satan unto the power of God.

> In whom the god of this world hath blinded the
> minds of them which believe not, lest the light
> of the glorious gospel of Christ, who is the
> image of God, should shine unto them.
>
> 2 Corinthians 4:4

The devil is the god of this world. His power includes the earth, nature, weather, nations, and the minds of them that don't believe. The devil offered this power to Jesus. He can only give what he has.

> And the devil, taking him up into an high
> mountain, shewed unto him all the kingdoms of
> the world in a moment of time.

> And the devil said unto him, All this power will
> I give *thee*, and the glory of them: for that is deliv-
> ered unto *me*, and to whomsoever I will I give it.
>
> Luke 4:5,6

Adam and Eve's unbelief delivered these powers to the devil. He has held them ever since. The powers that belong to the devil are great treasures of darkness meant to be built into the believing heart and found only in God's Word, The Bible.

> And I will give thee the treasures of darkness,
> and hidden riches of secret places, that thou
> mayest know that *I*, the LORD, which call *thee* by
> name, *am* the God of Israel.
>
> Isaiah 45:3

God desires to give the believing heart the treasures of light and darkness. The devil keeps them hidden. The less that is known, the more powerful he becomes. The Bible is the only book that reveals his limitations and boundaries. He does not know what you are thinking. He does not know the future. The devil is a respecter of persons. The devil does not have any power over the believing heart that lives by believing according to God's Word. His power can only be energized by unbelief. This is how he manipulates a course of believing. A course of long life, prosperity and good health can instantly turn to steal, kill, and destroy. When hate prevails in the believing heart, then the power of death can be energized at any time.

Forasmuch then as the children are partakers of flesh and blood, He also Himself likewise took part of the same; that through death He might destroy him that had the power of death, that is, the devil;

Hebrews 2:14

The devil has the power of death at this time. This power will be destroyed in the future. By God's grace and mercy, the believing heart lives. The Bible is filled with examples of believing hearts benefiting from God's grace and mercy and those who did not. One of the all-time great examples of this truth is Lot and his wife. Genesis, chapter 19 begins with two angels leading Lot and his family out of Sodom and Gomorrah just before it was destroyed.

And it came to pass, when they had brought *them* forth abroad, that He said, "Escape for thy life; look not behind thee, neither stay thou in all the plain; escape to the mountain lest thou be consumed."

And Lot said unto them, "Oh, not so, my Lord*:

Behold now, Thy servant hath found grace in Thy sight, and Thou hast magnified Thy mercy, which Thou hast shewed unto me in saving my life; and *I* cannot escape to the mountain, lest some evil take me, and I die:

Behold now, this city *is* near to flee unto, and *it is* a little one: Oh, let me escape thither, (*is it* not a little one?) and my soul shall live."

And he said unto him, "See, I have accepted thee concerning this thing also, that I will not overthrow this city, for the which thou hast spoken.

Haste thee, escape thither; for I cannot do anything till thou be come thither." Therefore the name of the city was called Zoar.

The sun was risen upon the earth when Lot entered into Zoar.

Then the LORD rained upon Sodom and upon Gomorrah brimstone and fire from the LORD out of heaven;

And He overthrew those cities, and all the inhabitants of the cities, and that which grew upon the ground.

But his wife looked back from behind him, and she became a pillar of salt.

Genesis 19:17-26

Lot escaped because he recognized God's grace and mercy was saving his life. He obeyed, allowing the love of God to prevail in his believing heart. His wife disobeyed and died. Hate prevailed in her heart, allowing the devil to take her life.

There is no fear in love; but perfect love casteth out fear: because fear hath torment. He that feareth is nor made perfect in love.

1 John 4:18

The love of God in the believing heart casts out fear. This is how it keeps itself protected by the middle section of the law of believing, God's grace and mercy. When hate prevails, the line is crossed over from God's grace and mercy to the negative side of the law of believing. Then the devil's power of death can be energized.

The Law of Believing (The Middle Section)

Love of God |    Love of God    | Hate

*Positive Side |  God's Grace/Mercy  | Negative Side*

*Pos Believing |   Pos/Neg Believing   | Negative Believing*

Power of God | Power of God devil  | Power of the devil

Life | Life/Death held in abeyance | Death

> Let us therefore come boldly unto the throne of
> grace, that we may obtain mercy, and find grace
> to help in time of need.
>
> Hebrews 4:16

God's grace and mercy is the middle section of the law of believing. It's the last line of defense against the power of death. What is in the believing heart determines who receives God's grace and mercy and who does not. All believing hearts are subject to the same spiritual world, spiritual powers, and spiritual laws. God is no respecter of persons. He is the greatest of all spiritual powers. Only he knows what we are thinking. Only he knows the future. God is the power of light and the devil is the power of darkness. God desires to give the believing heart the treasures of light and darkness. The devil desires to keep them hidden. Lot is an example of keeping the love of God in his believing heart. He obeyed and received with meekness God's grace and mercy, which saved his life. His wife did not. She allowed hate to prevail over her love for God, which energized the power of the devil. This allowed Satan to kill her. This is why Lot's course of believing continued and his wife's ended. God doesn't expect us to be perfect, but he does expect us to be faithful in keeping the greatest commandment: to love God with all our heart, soul, mind, and strength, and to love our neighbors as ourselves. Keeping the love of God in the believing heart, keeps Satan from prematurely ending a course of believing that has the opportunity to finish and obtain great rewards. This is the middle section of the law of believing, God's grace and mercy.

# CHAPTER 6

# THE POWER OF THE DEVIL

When the power of the devil becomes energized in the believing heart, spiritual darkness and death enters this world. This spiritual darkness results in fruit produced by the law of believing on the negative side. All fruit produced by the power of darkness has the shadow of death in it. No matter how good it looks, it eventually goes bad because of its source. To deceive the believing heart, the devil has to produce fruit resembling the power of God. This includes courses of unbelief resembling those who live by believing. All courses energized by the power of darkness lead to physical, mental, and spiritual captivity. Biblically, these are known as the courses of this world, as recorded in Ephesians, chapter 2. (Biblically walked means believed, and conversation means behavior).

> Wherein in time past ye walked according to the course of this world, according to the prince of the power of the air, the spirit that now worketh in the children of disobedience:
> Among whom also *we* all had our conversation in times past in the lusts of our flesh, fulfilling the desires of the flesh and of the mind; and were by nature the children of wrath, even as others.
>
> Ephesians 2:2,3

The devil as god of this world, commands all the courses of believing of this world. He is the prince of the power of the air. Outside of all these courses, only one alternative exists, God's Word. God's Word is not of this world. The Word of God is not to be of any private interpretation. Man did not will the Word of God into this world. The Word of God came into this world by believing hearts energized by the power of God.

> Knowing this first, that no prophecy of the Scripture is of any private interpretation.
> For the prophecy came not in old time by the will of man: but holy men of God spake *as they were* moved by the Holy Ghost.
>
> 2 Peter 1:20,21

The Word of God is not naturally built into the believing heart when we are born into this world. Without the Word of God to believe, the believing heart will naturally follow the courses of this world. Even believing hearts built by God's Word must retain it. This truth is found in 2 Peter, chapter 2.

> But it is happened unto them according to the true proverb, The dog *is* turned to his own vomit again; and the sow that was washed to her wallowing in the mire.
>
> 2 Peter 2:22

The vomit and wallowing mire that 2 Peter, chapter 2 is referring to are the courses of believing of this world that a believing heart returns to after having followed a course of believing set by God. Spiritually, only two courses of believing exist. The course of this world or God's Word. When hearts are blinded by the power of darkness, they only see the courses of this world. To them, God's Word is just one of many. The power of darkness blinding the minds who do not believe, can only be lifted by the power of God energizing in the believing heart. Only the acknowledgment of truth recovers the believing heart from the courses of this world.

> And the servant of the Lord must not strive; but be gentle unto all *men*, apt to teach, patient,
>
> In meekness instructing those that oppose themselves; if God peradventure will give them repentance to the acknowledging of the truth;
>
> And *that* they may recover themselves out of the snare of the devil, who are taken captive by him at *his* will.
>
> 2 Timothy 2:24-26

Only truth can set free the believing heart held captive by the devil. The courses of believing of this world are traps of the devil. When on these courses, the believing heart opposes itself. The courses of this world spiritually are vomit and sow mire. Teachers of God's Word must not struggle but be gentle unto all men, able to teach, be patient, and help believing hearts recover themselves from snares of the devil.

The power of the devil enters this world by the law of believing on the negative side. God's Word helps the believing heart understand how the power of darkness becomes energized in the believing heart. The law of believing on the negatives side is taught in James, chapter 1.

> Blessed *is* the man that endureth temptation: for when he is tried, he shall receive the crown of life, which the Lord hath promised to them that love Him.
> Let no man say when he is tempted, I am tempted of God: for God cannot be tempted with evil, neither tempteth *he* any man:
> But every man is tempted, when he is drawn away to his own lust, and enticed.
> Then when lust hath conceived, it bringeth forth sin: and sin, when it is finished, bringeth forth death.
>
> James 1:12-15

The law of believing separates the two spiritual powers. It shows how they energize and the type of fruit they produce. God cannot be tempted, neither does he tempt man. God is the spiritual power that rewards the believing heart. When we endure temptation, God rewards us with crowns of life.

Satan tempts man. The power of darkness draws the believing heart away by lust until it becomes enticed. This is an attack on the love of God. When lust conceives in the believing heart, hate has prevailed over the love of God and the power of darkness is energized. A course of believing set by Satan then begins. Hate drives the actions of believing hearts to produce fruit from the law of believing on the negative side. The fruit produced is sin. The finished work of sin ultimately brings death. This is the law of believing on the negative side.

*The Law of Believing (The Negative Side)*

<u>*Motivation: Hate*</u>

Satan Tempts by Lust

Enticed

<u>*Lust Conceives*</u>

The Power of The Devil Energized Resulting in Sin

This truth is first seen in the lives of Adam and Eve. It is the first time the power of the devil became energized in the believing heart and the reason sin affects our lives today. It's why the physical body dies. Genesis, chapter 3 is the record of these events.

> Now the serpent was more subtil than any beast of the field which the LORD God had made. And he said unto the woman, "Yea, hath God said, 'Ye shall not eat of every tree of the garden'?"
>
> Genesis 3:1

The devil begins tempting Eve's believing heart by questioning what God said and then tells a lie. The truth is what God said in Genesis, chapter 2:17, "But of the tree of the knowledge of good and evil, thou shalt not eat of it: for in the day that thou eatest thereof thou shalt surely die." To consume evil meant the power of the devil would become energized in their believing hearts bringing forth death. This example is how the devil begins to draw away the believing heart to a course of this world. The devil entices it to lust, which means going beyond need.

> And the Women said unto the serpent, "We may eat of the fruit of the trees of the garden:
> But of the fruit of the tree which *is* in the midst of the garden, God hath said, 'Ye shall not eat of it, neither shall ye touch it, lest ye die.'"
>
> Genesis 3:2,3

At this point, hate is building momentum to prevail over the love of God in Eve's believing heart. Once lust conceives, it brings forth sin. The finished work of sin is death.

> And the serpent said unto the woman, "Ye shall not surely die:
> For God doth know that in the day ye eat thereof, then your eyes shall be opened, and ye shall be as gods, knowing good and evil."
> And when the woman saw that the tree *was* good for food, and *it was* pleasant to the eyes, and a tree to be desired to make *one* wise, she took of the fruit thereof, and did eat, and gave also unto her hasband with her; and he did eat.
> And eyes of them both were opened, and they knew that *they were* naked; and they sewed fig leaves together, and made themselves aprons.
>
> Genesis 3:4-7

This is how the power of the devil energized in the believing hearts of Adam and Eve. They knew the spirit of God was conditional and would be lost if they sinned. When Adam was created, he had three basic parts. Body from the dust of the ground, soul life put into him, and spirit from God. What died on that day was the spirit of God in them. The body and soul remained intact. Adam and Eve confessed their sin unto God, and went on to live long lives living by believing, having the spirit of God conditionally. However from that point on, they could no longer stay in paradise and life changed in many ways. From this point on until Acts, chapter 2, the spirit of God was conditional upon all those who lived by believing. This is also marks the point in time when the need for a redeemer began, as eternal death became mankind's greatest enemy.

> For since by man came death, by man *came* also the resurrection of the dead.
> For as in Adam all die, even so in Christ shall all be made alive.
>
> 1 Corinthians 15:21,22

A redeemer was needed, one who could bring man back to God, back to his original state of body, soul, and spirit. Jesus Christ was that redeemer. Not until the time of the book of Acts, chapter 2, over 2,000 years ago did it become available again for man to become body, soul and spirit. Once holy spirit is received, it cannot be lost because of sin. The twelve apostles were the first to receive holy spirit, since the time of Adam and Eve lost it. Since that day when the twelve apostles first received holy spirit, it has been available to all those who will believe. Had the devil known this, he would not have crucified Jesus.

> Which none of the princes of this world knew: for had they known *it*, they would not have crucified the LORD of glory.
>
> 1 Corinthians 2:8

Spiritual darkness enters this world when the power of the devil is energized in the believing heart. When the power of the devil is energized, it always has a shadow of turning in it. There are only two spiritual courses of believing. The courses of this world are energized by the power of the devil. A course set by God is energized by the power of God. The courses of this world are traps of the devil. The believing heart can only recover from these courses by acknowledging truth. Truth energizes the power of God and removes spiritual blindness. The power of the devil enters this world by the law of believing. The devil tempts the believing heart away from truth by lust. Once lust is conceived in the believing heart it brings forth sin. The finished work of sin ends in death. Since creation, man was originally a three part being, body, soul, and spirit. Adam and Eve were the first to sin, resulting in the loss of spirit. This was the point in time when eternal death became mankind's greatest enemy, and also the need for a savior who could redeem mankind back to God began. Spirit was available but only conditional to those who lived by believing. Jesus Christ redeemed mankind back to God and holy spirit is available once again, but this time it cannot be lost by sin.

Had the devil understood God's plan of redemption, he would not have killed Jesus Christ. God desires eternal life for mankind and the devil desires eternal death. It's the power of the devil that brings spiritual darkness and death into this world.

# CHAPTER 7

# PAUL'S PATTERN OF BELIEVING

What matters most to God, is what is inside the believing heart. Only he can see inside. He sees all and knows all. This spiritual truth is beyond the knowledge of this world.

> That Christ may dwell in your hearts by faith; that ye, being rooted and grounded in love,
>
> May be able to comprehend with all saints what *is* the breadth, and length, and depth and height;
>
> And to know the love of Christ, which passeth knowledge, that ye might be filled with all the fulness of God.
>
> Ephesians 3:17-19

God's love is spiritual truth and goes beyond the knowledge of this world. It can only be comprehended when the power of God is energized in the believing heart, then the eyes of our spiritual understanding become enlightened, which reveals his love. The Apostle Paul's pattern of believing is all about understanding the depth of God's love.

All believing hearts are called by God to follow Paul's pattern of believing. His course shows how an evil and wicked believing heart can change. How sin can be forgiven, eternal life received, and a new course of believing can begin, set by God. It's a pattern of believing that makes the most of God's grace and mercy and finishes it. Paul summarizes his course of believing in 1 Timothy, chapter 1.

> And I thank Christ Jesus our LORD, Who hath enabled me, for that He counted me faithful, putting me into the ministry;
>
> Who was before a blasphemer, and a persecutor, and injurious: but I obtained mercy, because I did *it* ignorantly in unbelief.
>
> And the grace of our LORD was exceeding abundant with faith and love which is in Christ Jesus.
>
> This *is* a faithful saying, and worthy of all acceptation, that Christ Jesus came into the world to save sinners; of whom *I* am chief.
>
> Howbeit for this cause I obtained mercy, that in me first Jesus Christ might shew forth all longsuffering, for a pattern to them which should hereafter believe on Him to life everlasting.
>
> 1 Timothy 1:12-16

Paul went from being a blasphemer against God and a persecutor of those who lived by believing, to one who obtained mercy and life everlasting. This is Paul's pattern of believing. From birth and throughout his life, Paul's course of believing is recorded many times in God's Word for a purpose. It shows how a pattern of believing can change from a course of this world unto a course set by God. His life is an example that change is possible from any course of believing of this world. In Acts, chapter 22, Paul recalls his pattern of believing for Judeans entrenched in the same old course of believing that he once followed.

> "*I* am verily a man *which am* a Jew, born in Tarsus, *a city* in Cilicia, yet brought up in this city at the feet of Gamaliel, *and* taught according to the perfect manner of the law of the fathers, and was zealous toward God, as *ye* all are this day.
>
> And I persecuted this way unto the death, binding and delivering into prisons both men and women.
>
> As also the high priest doth bear me witness, and all the estate of the elders: from whom also I received letters unto the brethren, and went to Damascus, to bring them which were there bound unto Jerusalem, for to be punished.
>
> And it came to pass, that as I made my journey, and was come nigh unto Damascus about noon, suddenly there shone from heaven a great light round about me.
>
> And I fell unto the ground, and heard a voice saying unto me, Saul[refers to Paul], Saul, why persecutes thou Me?'
>
> And *I* answered, "Who art Thou, Lᴏʀᴅ?" And He said unto me, '*I* am Jesus of Nazareth, Whom *thou* persecutest.'
>
> And they that were with me saw indeed the light, and were afraid; but they heard not the voice of Him That spake to me.

And I said, 'What shall I do, Lord?' And the Lord said unto me, 'Arise and go into Damascus; and there it shall be told thee of all things which are appointed for thee to do.'

And when I could not see for the glory of that light, being led by the hand of them that were with me, I came into Damascus.

And one Ananias, a devout man according to the law, having a good report of all the Jews which dwelt *there*,

Came unto me, and stood, and said unto me, 'Brother Saul, receive thy sight.' And the same hour *I* looked up upon him.

And he said, 'The God of our fathers hath chosen thee, that thou shouldest know His will and see that Just One, and shouldest hear the voice of His mouth.

For thou shalt be His witness unto all men of what thou hast seen and heard.

And now why tarriest thou? arise, and be baptized, and wash away thy sins, calling on the name of the Lord.'

And it came to pass, that, when I was come again to Jerusalem, even while I prayed in the temple, I was in a trance;

And saw Him saying unto me, 'Make haste, and get thee quickly out of Jerusalem: for they will not receive thy testimony concerning Me.'

And *I* said, "Lord, *they* know that *I* imprisoned and beat in every synagogue them that believed on Thee:

And when the blood of Thy martyr Stephen was shed, *I* also was standing by, and consenting unto his death, and kept the raiment of them that slew him.'

> And He said unto me, 'Depart: for *I* will send
> thee far hence unto the Gentiles.'"

Acts 22:3-21

Paul's course of believing was changed by Jesus.
This is how all courses can become changed. A course
of believing set by Satan that commits the unforgivable
sin is the only one that cannot be changed (Mark 3:28,
29). Acts chapter 9 is another record of Paul's pattern
of believing, just before he leaves for Damascus and his
believing hearts first experiences at living by believing.

> And Saul, yet breathing out threatening and slaugh-
> ter against the disciples of the Lord, went unto the
> high priest,
>
> And desired of him letters to Damascus to
> the synagogues, that if he found any of this way,
> whether they were men or women, he might
> bring them bound unto Jerusalem.
>
> And as he journeyed, he came near Damascus:
> and suddenly there shined round about him a
> light from heaven:
>
> And he fell to the earth, and heard a voice
> saying unto him, "Saul[refers to apostle Paul],
> Saul, why persecutes thou Me?"
>
> And he said, "Who art Thou, Lord?" And
> the Lord said, "*I* am Jesus Whom *thou* persecut-
> est: *it is* hard for thee to kick against the pricks."
>
> And he trembling and astonished said,
> "Lord, what wilt Thou have me to do?" And the
> Lord *said* unto him, "Arise, and go into the city,
> and it shall be told thee what thou must do."
>
> And the men which journeyed with him stood
> speechless, hearing a voice, but seeing no man.

And Saul arose from the earth; and when his eyes were opened, he saw no man: but they led him by the hand, and brought *him* into Damascus. And he was three days without sight, and neither did eat nor drink.

And there was a certain disciple at Damascus, named Ananias; and to him said the LORD in a vision, "Ananias." And he said, "*Behold, I am here,* LORD."

And the LORD *said* unto him, "Arise and go into the street which is called Straight, and enquire in the house of Judas for one called Saul, of Tarsus: for, behold, he prayeth,

And hath seen in a vision a man named Ananias coming in, and putting *his* hand on him, that he might receive his sight."

Then Ananias answered, "LORD, I have heard by many of this man, how much evil he hath done to Thy saints at Jerusalem:

And here he hath authority from the chief priests to bind all that call on Thy name."

But the LORD said unto him, "Go thy way: for *he* is a chosen vessel unto Me, to bear My name before the Gentiles, and kings, and the children of Israel:

For *I* will shew him how great things he must suffer [biblically, means endure] for My name's sake."

And Ananias went his way, and entered into the house; and putting his hands on him said,

"Brother Saul, the LORD, *even* Jesus, That appeared unto thee in the way as thou camest, hath sent me, that thou mightest receive thy sight, and be filled with the Holy Ghost."

And immediately there fell from his eyes as it had been scales: and he received sight forthwith, and arose, and was baptized.

And when he had received meat, he was strengthened. Then was Saul certain days with the disciples which were at Damascus.

And straightway he preached Christ in the synagogues, that *he* is the Son of God.

But all that heard *him* were amazed, and said: "Is not this he that destroyed them which called on this name in Jersusalem, and came hither for that intent, that he might bring them bound unto the chief priests?"

But Saul increased the more in strength, and confounded the Jews which dwelt at Damascus, proving this is very Christ.

And after that many days were fulfilled, the Jews took counsel to kill him:

But their laying await was known of Saul. And they watched the gates day and night to kill him.

Then the disciples took him by night, and let *him* down by the wall in a basket.

And when Saul was come to Jerusalem, he assayed to join himself to the disciples: but they were all afraid of him, and believed not that he was a disciple.

But Barnabas took him, and brought *him* to the apostles, and declared unto them how he had seen the Lord in the way, and that He had spoken to him, and how he had preached boldly at Damascus in the name of Jesus.

And he was with them coming in and going out at Jerusalem.

Acts 9:1-28

Paul went from threatening and slaughtering those who lived by believing to preaching Christ. Once on God's course, Paul's life becomes endangered by those on the course of believing set by Satan. The same course he once followed. In Philippians, chapter 3, Paul talks about this course. He concludes that all those things that used to be gain to him, meaning all his life's accomplishments before accepting Christ, were dung when compared to a course of believing set by God.

> Though *I* might also have confidence in flesh. If any other man thinketh that he hath whereof he might trust in the flesh, *I* more:
> Circumcised the eighth day, of the stock of Israel, *of* the tribe of Benjamin, an Hebrew of the Hebrews: as touching the law, a Pharisee;
> Concerning zeal, persecuting the church; touching the righteousness which is in the law, blameless.
> But what things were gain to me, those I counted loss for Christ.
> Yea doubtless, and I count all things *but* loss for the excellency of the knowledge of Christ Jesus my LORD: for Whom I have suffered the loss of all things, and do count them *but* dung, that I may win Christ,
> And be found in Him, not having mine own righteousness, which is of the law, but that which is through the faith of Christ, the righteousness which is of God by faith:
>
> Philippians 3:4-9

When changing from a course of believing in this world to a course of believing set by God, a spiritual change needs to happen first. The spiritual change Paul went through was to become filled with holy spirit. Ananias, who lived by believing, obeyed God when asked to help Paul. After Ananias believed through his own fears about Paul, God gave him two jobs. First, Ananias ministered healing unto Paul to receive sight. Next, Paul needed to be filled with holy spirit. 1 Corinthians, chapter 15 records how Ananias completed this second job. This is the pattern all believing hearts need to follow to become filled with holy spirit.

> Moreover, brethren, I declare unto you the gospel which I preached unto you, which also ye have received, and wherein ye stand;
>
> By which also ye are saved, if ye keep in memory what I preached unto you, unless ye have believed in vain.
>
> For I delivered unto you first of all that which I also received, how that Christ died for our sins according to the scriptures,
>
> And that He was buried, and that He rose again the third day according to the scriptures:
>
> And that he was seen of Cephas, than of the twelve:
>
> After that, He was seen of above five hundred brethren at once, of whom the greater part remain unto this present, but some are fallen asleep.
>
> After that, He was seen of James; then of all the apostles.
>
> And last of all He was seen of me also, as of one born out of due time.
>
> For *I* am the least of the apostles, that am not meet to be called an apostle, because I persecuted the church of God.

> But by the grace of God I am what I am:
> and His grace which *was bestowed* upon me was
> not in vain; but I laboured more abundantly than
> they all: yet not *I*, but the grace of God which
> was with me.

> 1 Corinthians 15:1-10

The first thing Paul received from Ananias after regaining his sight was how Christ died for our sins, was buried, and that he rose again the third day, according to the scriptures. Paul believed this truth regarding Christ from God's Word. This is Paul's pattern of believing of how to receive holy spirit. Paul grew from this initial teaching from Ananias, and went on to develop his own God inspired teachings of how to receive holy spirit. Romans, chapter 10, records how Paul taught others to receive holy spirit.

> That if thou shalt confess with thy mouth the
> LORD Jesus, and shalt believe in thine heart that
> God hath raised Him from the dead, thou shalt
> be saved.
> For with the heart man believeth unto right-
> eousness; and with the mouth confession is
> made unto salvation.

> Romans 10:9,10

This is the pattern of Paul's believing heart that all subsequent believing hearts are called by God to follow, to receive holy spirit. This is how sin is forgiven and eternal life received.

Death and life *are* in the power of the tongue:
And they that love it shall eat the fruit[biblically
fruit means the outcomes of the law of believing]
thereof.

Proverbs 18:21

Death and life are in the power of the tongue of the
believing heart. Both energize spiritual power. Paul's
pattern of believing is how to receive eternal life. When
holy spirit is received, the power of God has been energized. This means that the river of God's knowledge and
God's wisdom have become one in the believing heart.
The new river that is formed is the wisdom of the power
of God and spiritual understanding. God's knowledge is
making Jesus LORD and that God has raised him from
the dead. God's wisdom is confessing with the mouth
and believing in the heart.

And this is the record, that God hath given to us
eternal life, and this life is in His Son.
He that hath the Son hath life; *and* he that
hath not the Son of God hath not life.
The things have I written unto you that
believe on the name of the Son of God; that ye
may know that ye have eternal life, and that ye
may believe on the name of the Son of God.

1 John 5:11-13

Biblically, this is known as being *born again*. It's a new
birth of incorruptible seed, eternal life that can never be
lost. The first birth into this world is with corruptible seed.

> Being born again, not of corruptible seed, but of
> incorruptible, by the word of God, which liveth
> and abideth for ever.

1 Peter 1:23

When the believing heart confesses that Jesus is LORD and that God raised him from the dead; the power of God energizes the believing heart and receives righteousness, justification, sanctification, redemption, and the ministry of reconciliation. At that moment, the believing heart is put on a course of believing set by God. The believing heart must learn to live by believing to stay on this course. Sin puts the believing heart back on course of this world; however, the incorruptible seed of holy spirit cannot be lost. Confession of sin before God puts the believing heart back on a course set by God. This is how Paul spiritually changed from the courses of this world to a course set by God. It's how all believing hearts change spiritually from the courses of this world and begin a new course set by God.

> For I am not ashamed of the gospel of Christ: for it
> is the power of God unto salvation to everyone that
> believeth; to the Jew first, and also to the Greek.
>
> For therein is the righteousness of God revealed
> from faith to faith: as it is written, "The just shall
> live by faith[biblically faith means believing]."

Romans 1:16,17

Paul made the most of God's grace and mercy. He pursued a course to become a master believer. He knew

Peter, James and all the other apostles. However, Paul had one quality that separated him from the others. He refused to allow the grace of God in his life to be in vain, indeed, he labored more abundantly than all others in his pursuit to live by believing and helping others. God's grace was a mighty core value in Paul's believing heart. This is how he became the leader of the first century Christian Church. God entrusted him to write the book of Romans, 1 Corinthians, 2 Corinthians, Galatians, Ephesians, Philippians, Colossians, 1 Thessalonians, and 2 Thessalonians. These are specifically addressed to those who will follow Paul's pattern of believing and live by believing. These books teach the believing heart how to become strong in the LORD and the power of his might. This is the spiritual milk and meat that is meant for today's believing heart. This teaches us how to discern which is spiritually good and evil, and how to finish the course of believing set by God. It's from these books that the believing heart learns that Christ is the power of God to all believing hearts that will believe.

> **Romans**: The foundational teachings and principles of God's accomplishments in Jesus Christ's life, death, and resurrection from the dead for all mankind.

> **1 and 2 Corinthians**: Reproof for practical errors of not adhering to the foundational teachings in the book of Romans.

> **Galatians**: Correction for doctrinal error of not adhering to the teachings in Romans.

**Ephesians**: The great mystery of the gospel of Christ revealed. Judean and gentile are as one new man in Christ with spiritual identification as seated in the heavenlies above all the rulers of darkness of this world with Christ by God.

**Philippians**: Reproof for practical error of not adhering to the teachings in Ephesians.

**Colossians**: Correction for doctrinal error of not adhering to the teaching in Ephesians.

**1, 2 Thessalonians**: The gathering of the Church of Grace to Christ.

Paul also wrote the leadership books, 1 and 2 Timothy, Titus, and Philemon. The book of Hebrews is a teaching of the good news of Christ but is addressed to those who are entrenched in the Judean course of believing. These believing hearts had spiritually changed their courses of believing but had trouble staying the new course set by God and were being tempted to go back to their old course. Fourteen books were inspired by God but written by the hand of the Apostle Paul.

The book of Acts and Paul's fourteen books are the record of his own spiritual growth and understanding, which he taught others. Only Paul's teachings helps us understand the spiritual riches that come after the knowledge of Jesus Christ crucified. This knowledge reveals our spiritual identification with God, as well as our sonship rights. As sons and daughters of God, our true standing is being seated in the heavenlies with Satan under our feet.

When Christ died we died with him. When Christ arose from the dead, we arose with him. When Christ sat down at the right hand of God, our spiritual identification is to be seated with him, far above the devil and his evil spirit kingdom of this world. Also, the only listing of the nine manifestations of holy spirit in the Bible, is found in 1 Corinthians, chapter 12. Chapters 13 and 14 teach how the gift of the holy spirit profits the individual and the church. The book of Acts records how these teachings were applied by the first century Christian Church. Ephesians records the great mystery, how Judeans and Gentiles are called to be one body, in Christ. Thessalonians records how Christ will return and gather the church, and forever be with the LORD. All this great revelation and more, was given by God to the believing heart of the Apostle Paul.

God knew that Paul's pattern and example of believing was the best for all believing hearts to follow. Paul at one time was entrenched in an evil course of believing, which was dead in sin. All believing hearts are dead in sin and follow the courses of this world before spiritually changing courses. Paul needed help from others to learn from the scriptures how to be filled with holy spirit. All believing hearts since then needed help from others who live by believing and on how to receive holy spirit, just like Paul. Paul made the most of God's grace in his life, and labored to become a master believer. All believing hearts need to follow Paul's pattern of believing and make the most of God's grace, and labor to become a master believer, just like Paul. Paul kept the good fight until the end of his life. He finished his course of believing by keeping in sight the future rewards and the return of Christ. All believing hearts need to stay their course of believing set by God, and keep the good fight until the end, just like Paul.

> For *I* am now ready to be offered, and the time of my departure is at hand.
>
> I have fought the a good fight, I have finished *my* course, I have kept the faith:
>
> Henceforth there is laid up for me a crown of righteousness, which the LORD, the righteous Judge, shall give me at that day: and not to me only, but unto all them also that love His appearing.
>
> 2 Timothy 4:6-8

Only God knows what is in the believing heart. Only he knows who will or will not change from the devil's courses. Paul's pattern of believing reveals that change is possible, even from the most evil of courses. This is God's love, a love and knowledge that goes beyond this world. Confessing in the believing heart that Jesus is LORD and that God raised him from the dead is how to become filled with holy spirit. This is how Paul changed from the devil's course of believing unto a course set by God. It's how all believing hearts can change to a course set by God. Once changed, Paul realized that the courses of this world are dung. He clearly recognized this was God's grace in his life and he took full advantage of it, laboring to become a great master believer. Paul became the leader of the first century Christian Church. God entrusted to Paul's believing heart fourteen of His books.

These included the seven Christian Church Epistles and four Christian leadership epistles, which are the milk and meat for today's believing heart. He took up the good fight until the very end of his life. He finished his course with the view of the future rewards that would be given to him and to all those who follow his pattern of believing when Christ returns.

# CHAPTER 8

# WHAT'S AHEAD

Knowing what is coming ahead of time has its advantages, especially when it comes to God's Word and the believing heart. "The Parable of the Sower and the Seed" teaching by Jesus illustrates this advantage. This one teaching provides an inside look into the spirit world, the significance of God's Word, and the relationship the two have with the believing heart. It gives us a glimpse of what lies ahead for all believing hearts, once the Word of God is found.

> And when much people were gathered together, and were come to Him out of every city, he spake by a parable:
> A sower went out to sow his seed: and as he sowed, some fell by the way side; and it was trodden down, and the fowls of the air devoured it.
> And some fell upon a rock; and as soon as it was sprung up, it withered away, because it lacked moisture.
> And some fell among thorns; and the thorns sprang up with it, and choked it.

And other fell on good ground, and sprang up, and bare fruit an hundredfold." And when He had said these things, He cried, "He that hath ears to hear, let him hear."

And His disciples asked Him, saying, "What might this parable be?"

And He said, "Unto you it is given to know the mysteries of the kingdom of God: but to others in parables; that seeing they might not see, and hearing they might not understand.

Now the parable is this: The seed is the word of God.

Those by the way side are they that hear; then cometh the devil, and taketh away the word out of their hearts, lest they should believe and be saved.

They on the rock *are they*, which, when they hear, receive the word with joy; and these have no root, which for a while believe, and in time of temptation fall away.

And that which fell among thorns are they, which, when they have heard, go forth, and are choked with cares and riches and pleasures of *this* life, and bring no fruit to perfection.

But that on the good ground are they, which in an honest and good heart, having heard the word, keep *it*, and bring forth fruit with patience.

Luke 8:4-15

This great teaching by Jesus reveals the truth about this world and what matters most. Singled out is the number one thing that changes this world. This one thing has been the difference between the human race being wiped off the face of the earth, and the world we enjoy today. That one great thing is the greatest treasure of the believing heart, God's Word. When God's Word becomes believed it energizes the power of God into this world. It brings light and life into a world filled with darkness. Currently, a world where the devil is god and his courses of believing is all that is known.

Only four courses of believing exist in this world to follow. Three of these courses are set by Satan. First, hearts that are so hard that they cannot receive God's Word. Secondly, hearts that lack the ability to grasp the depth of God's Word. Third, believing hearts that became so choked with the cares of this world and the pleasures of this life that they cannot bring the consistent power of God into this world. The fourth and best course is set by God. This is a course where the believing heart becomes good ground and produces fruit. Good ground believing hearts are consistently producing fruit from the positive side of the law of believing. This is evident of a mature, believing heart. A heart that is strong in the LORD and in the power of his might. God desirers this course for all men.

> Who will have all men to be saved, and to come
> unto the knowledge of the truth.
>
> 1 Timothy 2:4

When the power of God enters this world, it causes great disruption to the devil's kingdom. In Luke, chapter 10, Jesus talks about this disruption and reminds the seventy to stay humble by remembering the greatest work of God in their lives is that their names are written in heaven.

> And the seventy returned again with joy, saying, "LORD, even the devils are subject unto us through Thy name."
> And He said unto them, "I beheld Satan as lightning fall from heaven.
> Behold, I give unto you power to tread on serpents and scorpions, and over all the power of the enemy: and nothing shall by any means hurt you.
> Notwithstanding in this rejoice not, that the spirits are subject unto you; but rather rejoice, because your names are written in heaven."
>
> Luke 10:17-20

Hearing and keeping the Word of God within the believing heart, is how it becomes the good ground producing fruit. Becoming born again is just the beginning of a new and exciting life. We are then no longer spiritually blind and the believing heart can see the treasures of God's Word. This is the point in time when the believing heart can be built by the treasures of God's Word. We change from a course of believing that is of this world, unto a course set by God. The devil knows these eternal stakes are always at risk, which is why he attacks the Word of God every chance he gets.

When the believing heart follows a course set by Satan, it is deceived and spiritually blinded. Lies and deception dismantle the walls of God's Word, which protect the believing heart, opening it up to attack. Proverbs, chapter 4 describes this kind of believing heart.

> I went by the field of the slothful, And by the vineyard of the man void of understanding;
>
> And, lo, it was all grown over with thorns, *And* nettles had covered the face thereof, And the stone wall thereof was broken down.
>
> Then *I* saw, *and* considered *it* well: I looked upon *it*, and received instruction.
>
> *Yet* a little sleep, a little slumber, A little folding of the hands to sleep:
>
> So shall thy poverty come *as* one that traveled; And thy want as an armed man.
>
> Proverbs 24:30-34

The courses of believing of this world will grow weeds in the believing heart. The stone wall of the love of God becomes broken down, giving way to hate. The believing heart becomes spiritually asleep, and is not able to recognize what lies ahead. When the day of evil comes, it desires God's protection. It's just like the foolish man whose heart is built on the sand. He cannot escape the course of believing he has been following on the day of evil, just as a woman who cannot stop in the middle of delivering a baby. These are the kind of weak believing hearts that cannot stop the evil spiritual storm about to strike. Once the law of believing on the negative side is energized by the power of the devil, negative results will follow.

## The Law of Believing (Negative Side)

### *Motivation: Hate*

### *Lies and Deception—Stone Wall Broken Down*

## The Power of the devil—Negative Results

This is why the Word of God is the greatest treasure that we can build into our believing hearts. It holds the potential to become the power of God in this world. "The Parable of the Sower and the Seed" is a description of the spiritual war that takes place in the believing heart over the Word of God. It's a war over courses of believing, a war of power that will be energized in this world between the power of God or the power of the devil. It is also a war over values, where hate in its many shapes and forms naturally attacks God's Word, most specifically the love of God.

> A good man out of the good treasure of his heart bringeth forth that which is good; and an evil man out of the evil treasure of his heart bringeth forth that which is evil: for of the abundance of the heart his mouth speaketh.
>
> Luke 6:45

Good and evil can always be traced back to what is inside the believing heart. This is why everything matters in the heart all the time. Every moment, every thought, every action, everything that comes out of the mouth affects the heart. Everything matters all the time, because the believing heart is spiritual and lives

by believing. Once a thought becomes a treasure of the
believing heart, spiritual power has the potential to be
energized by the law of believing. This is why the type of
treasures built into the believing heart is always significant. These treasures eventually determine which spiritual power will be brought into this world and which
kind of results.

> For though we walk in the flesh, we do not war
> after the flesh:
> (For the weapons of our warfare *are* not
> carnal, but mighty through God to the pulling
> down of strong holds;)
> Casting down imaginations, and every high
> thing that exalteth itself against the knowl-
> edge of God, and bringing into captivity every
> thought to the obedience of Christ;
>
> 2 Corinthians 10:3-5

The war for good treasure over evil within the
believing heart is a series of battles that goes on during
the entire course of believing. This war is won when
the course of believing is finished in this world. The
sin nature of the believing heart is to believe according to the courses of this world and hold evil treasure.
All believing hearts come into this world built this way.
In Romans, chapter 12, this war is called the renewing
of the mind. Instead of conforming to the courses of
believing of this world, the believing heart must prove
to itself what the good, acceptable, and perfect will of
God is.

And be not conformed to this world: but be ye transformed by the renewing of your mind, that ye may prove what is that good, acceptable, and perfect, will of God.

Romans 12:2

The spiritual growth process, from the milk of God's word unto its meat, is a process of change. All believing hearts have to pull down the strongholds of unbelief to become spiritually minded. Not all strongholds are the same within the believing heart. It takes commitment, focus, and diligence to win. Above all, it takes faithfulness. To align every thought according to God's Word takes time, effort, and a lot of daily work. The more work you put into it, the easier it becomes to renew the mind. The power of God eventually will work in you and fear will be cast out. God doesn't hold us accountable to being perfect, but he expects us to be faithful.

That we *henceforth* be no more children, tossed to and fro, and carried about with every wind of doctrine, by the sleight of men, *and* cunning caftiness, whereby they lie in wait to deceive;

But speaking the truth in love, may grow up into Him in all things, Which is the Head, *even* Christ.

Ephesians 4:14,15

A believing heart built by the milk of God's Word will struggle. It must grow up spiritually by the meat of God's Word to withstand fiery darts of unbelief. A believing heart that bounces back and forth from good and evil is immature and childlike. These are believing hearts who bring immature fruit into this world. This is a course of believing of this world. Satan watches those who feed on the milk and the meat. As the prince and power of the air, he originates the winds of doctrines that are contrary to God's Word. This power becomes energized by the evil treasure within believing hearts of those who are skillful at deceiving the heart. The weak and faint hearted will be devoured by the devil and will become conformed to the sinful courses of believing of this world.

> Be sober, be vigilant; because your adversary the devil, as a roaring lion, walketh about, seeking whom he may devour:
> Whom resist steadfast in the faith, knowing that the same afflictions are accomplished in your brethern that are in the world.
> But the God of all grace, Who hath called us unto His eternal glory by Christ Jesus, after that ye have suffered a while, make you perfect, stablish, strengthen, settle *you*.
>
> 1 Peter 5:8-10

Being sober, vigilant, and resisting the devil is how these battles within the believing heart are won. Suffering afflictions and persecutions are attacks the devil will bring to those who will live by believing. Each battle presents the opportunity for the believing heart to become stronger and wiser. This is like the believing heart that Solomon described, which becomes established by understanding. These hearts become skillful at receiving from God. The law of believing on the positive side is established in this believing heart. It's a believing heart filled with God's knowledge, wisdom, and understanding.

## The Law of Believing (Positive Side)

*Motivation: Love of God*

God's Knowledge

*God's Wisdom*

God's Understanding—The Power of God—Positive Results

In Ephesians, chapter 6, the apostle Paul describes what is inside the strong believing heart. It gives a picture of the believing heart nourished by the meat of God's Word. This is what a believing heart looks like that can finish a course of believing set by God and receive a full reward.

> Finally, my brethren, be strong in the LORD, and in the power of His might.
>
> Put on the whole armour of God, that ye may be able to stand against the wiles of the devil.
>
> For we wrestle not against flesh and blood, but against principalities, against powers, against the rulers of the darkness of this world, against spiritual wickedness in high *places*.
>
> Wherefore take unto you the whole armour of God, that ye may be able to withstand in the evil day, having done all, to stand.

Stand therefore, having your loins girt about with truth, and having on the breastplate of righteousness;

And your feet shod with the preparation of the gospel of peace;

Above all, taking the shield of faith, wherewith ye shall be able to quench all the fiery darts of the wicked.

And take the helmet of salvation, and the sword of the Spirit, which is the word of God:

Praying always with all prayer and supplication in the Spirit, and watching thereunto with all perseverance and supplication for all saints,

Ephesians 6:10-18

To finish the course of believing set by God, the believing heart must become strong in the power of His might. This requires putting on all the armor of God within the believing heart to withstand the methods devised by the devil that are designed to dismantle the Word of God. God wants the believing heart to stand through these attacks by commitment, by the power of holy spirit and by a reflexive knowledge of God's Word that is prepared for action. Above all, God wants the believing heart to build a shield and helmet within the heart that quenches all the fiery darts of the devil. This kind of believing heart is prepared to persevere unto the finish line, and also pray for the needs of others who live by believing.

Knowing what is ahead is a great advantage. "The Parable of the Sower and the Seed" does this for the believing heart. Once the Word of God has been received, then the best preparations can be made to become and remain the *good ground* believing heart. Only the Word of God, when believed, has the ability to bring the power of God into this world. Only by the Word of God can the believing heart stand against all the fiery darts of the devil. This is why the devil does everything possible to stop its development. It's the Word of God that gives us this great advantage; thereby, alerting us to the truth of what we all are up against, and what it will take to win. This is what's ahead, and now it's up to you. What course will you take?

# CHAPTER 9

# FINISHERS

The greatest words ever spoken in the history of mankind are, "It is finished." These words were spoken by Jesus just before he died on the cross. John, chapter 19 records these final moments.

> After this, Jesus, knowing that all things were now accomplished, that the scripture might be fulfilled, saith, "I thirst."
>
> Now there was set a vessel full of vinegar: and they filled a spunge with vinegar, and put it upon hyssop, and put *it* to His mouth.
>
> When Jesus therefore had received the vinegar, He said, "It is finished:" and He bowed His head, and gave up the ghost.
>
> John 19:28-30

What was finished? God's plan for the redemption of mankind was finished. Jesus had destroyed the works of the devil, which includes death. That's why, "It is finished" are the greatest words ever spoken.

> For this purpose the Son of god was manifested, that He might destroy the works of the devil.
>
> 1 John 3:8b

"It is finished" is what every believing heart should look forward to saying at the end of a course of believing set by God. The Apostle Paul understood this great truth, and once he learned how to live by believing, his whole life became focused and multiplied by it.

> But none of these things move me, neither count I my life dear unto myself, so that I might finish my course with joy, and the ministry, which I have received of the LORD Jesus, to testify the gospel of the grace of God.
>
> Acts 20:24

All believing hearts that live by believing should have their lives focused by, "It is finished." It's the meat of God's Word, meant to get the believing heart to the finish line.

> Jesus saith unto them, "My meat is to do the will of Him That sent me, and to finish His work.
>
> John 4:34

Finishing God's work is what life is all about. Once the believing heart begins to live by believing, a special course of believing becomes set by God to finish. A course of believing that looks forward to that day and saying like Paul, "I have fought a good fight, I have finished my course." This is what a real life is all about. Can there be anything more thrilling than living a course of believing set by God? The Bible has one special chapter devoted to finishers. When the believing heart feels wearied and faint, all it has to do is consider the finishers of the past, those who ran the course set by God, finishing in believing. Only the Bible has such a list. What happens next is that the believing heart discovers that it is surrounded by a great cloud of witnesses, who fought the good fight and finished. It is a witness to all believing hearts that a course set by God can be finished, and their lives prove it. (Biblically faith in this usage means believing).

> Wherefore seeing *we* also are compassed about with so great a cloud of witnesses, let us lay aside every weight, and the sin which doth so easily beset *us*, and let us run with patience the race that is set before us.
>
> Looking unto Jesus the Author and Finisher of *our* faith, Who for the joy that was set before Him endured the cross, despising the shame, and is set down at the right hand of the throne of God.
>
> For consider Him That endured such contradiction of sinners against Himself, lest ye be wearied and faint in your minds.
>
> Hebrews 12:1-3

Jesus Christ is the greatest finisher of all time. This makes his course of believing especially significant. He finished the course that God had set before his believing heart with joy. Similarly, Paul talked about this joy that God has set before all believing hearts of today, saying, "Henceforth there is laid up for me a crown of righteousness, which the LORD, the righteous Judge, shall give me at that day: and not to me only, but unto all them also that love His appearing." This joy is the hope of Christ's return. It is the anchor of the believing heart that keeps it on course to finish.

But I would not have you to be ignorant, brethren, concerning them which are asleep, that ye sorrow not, even as others which have no hope.

For if we believe that Jesus died and rose again, even so them also which sleep in Jesus will God bring with Him.

For this we say unto you by the word of the LORD, that *we* which are alive *and* remain unto the coming of the LORD, shall not prevent them which are asleep.

For the LORD Himself shall descend from heaven with a shout, with the voice of the archangel, and with the trump of God: and the dead in Christ shall rise first:

Then *we* which are alive, *and* remain, shall be caught up together with them in the clouds, to meet the LORD in the air: and so shall we ever be with the LORD.

Wherefore comfort one another with these words.

1 Thessalonians 4:13-18

All believing hearts who finish, have the great joy of the hope of Christ's return built into them. This keeps it from straying unto courses of this world. It is also God's comfort which strengthens us to the finish. Like a long distance runner, finishing is dependent on traveling light. The believing heart can be its own worst enemy and carry sin that has already been forgiven. Sin will disrupt the course and keep it from finishing. The believing heart must learn to lay aside the weight of sin to run the course of God's Word. To lay aside, means to forget and reach forward with energized works of believing.

Sin brings the power of the devil into this world, which also must be endured. The believing hearts that follow the courses of this world contradict those who live by believing. All unbelief brings spiritual darkness into this world and must be patiently endured. Patiently enduring unbelief that can develop within the believing heart, and within others, is done by nourishment from God's Word. When the believing heart believes God's Word, the power of God becomes energized, it does not only bring light and life into this world, but also into the believing heart. This is the spiritual strength all believing hearts need to finish their course. Building God's Word into the believing heart is the work of staying the course. A believing heart that is strong enough to finish, will look like the fully equipped Roman soldier ready for war, as described by Paul in Ephesians, chapter 6. This is the kind of believing heart found in Jesus, and also in the list of finishers in Hebrews, chapter 11. The key to understanding this chapter is the word *faith*. This word is used many times in this chapter. The proper translation of this word should be "believing." When faith is understood to mean believing, then the great truth of finishing a course of believing set by God comes to light.

> Now faith is the substance of things hoped for, the evidence of things not seen.
>
> For by it the elders obtained a good report.
>
> Through faith we understand that the worlds were framed by the word of God, so that things which are seen were not made of things which do appear.

By faith Abel offered unto God a more excellent sacrifice than Cain, by which he obtained witness that he was righteous, God testifying of his gifts: and by it he being dead yet speaketh.

By faith Enoch was translated that he should not see death; and was not found because God had translated him: for before his translation he had this testimony, that he pleased God.

But without faith *it is* impossible to please *Him*: for he that cometh to God must believe that He is, and *that* He is a rewarder of them that diligently seek Him.

By faith Noah, being warned of God of things not seen as yet, moved with fear, prepared an ark to the saving of his house; by the which he condemned the world, and became heir of the righteousness which is by faith.

By faith Abraham, when he was called to go out into a place which he should after receive for an inheritance, obeyed; and he went out, not knowing whither he went.

By faith he sojourned in the land of promise, as *in* a strange *country*, dwelling in tabernacles with Isaac and Jacob, the heirs with him of the same promise:

For he looked for a city which hath foundations, whose builder and maker *is* God.

Through faith also Sara herself received strength to conceive seed, and was delivered of a child when she was past age, because she judged Him faithful Who had promised.

Therefore sprang there even of one, and him as good as dead, *so many* as the stars of the sky in multitude, and as the sand which is by the sea shore innumerable.

These all died in faith, not having received the promises, but having seen them afar off, and were persuaded of *them*, and embraced *them*, and confessed that they were strangers and pilgrims on the earth.

For they that say such things declare plainly that they seek a country.

And truly if they had been mindful of that *country* from whence they came out, they might have had opportunity to have returned.

But now they desire a better *country*, that is, an heavenly: wherefore God is not ashamed to be called *their* God: for He hath prepared for them a city.

By faith Abraham, when he was tried, offered up Isaac: and he that had received the promises offered up his only begotten *son*,

Of whom it was said, That in Isaac shall they seed be called:"

Accounting that God *was* able to raise *him* up, even from the dead; from whence also he received him in a figure.

By faith Isaac blessed Jacob and Esau concerning things to come.

By faith Jacob, when he was dying, blessed both the sons of Joseph; and worshipped, *leaning* upon the top of his staff.

By faith Joseph, when he died, made mention of the departing of the children of Israel; and gave commandment concerning his bones.

By faith Moses, when he was born, was hid three months of his parents, because they saw *he was* a proper child; and they were not afraid of the king's commandment.

By faith Moses, when he was come to years, refused to be called the son of Pharaoh's daughter;

Choosing rather to suffer affliction with the people of God, than to enjoy the pleasures of sin for a season;

Esteeming the reproach of Christ greater riches than the treasures in Egypt: for he had respect unto the recompence of the reward.

By faith he forsook Egypt, not fearing the wrath of the king: for he endured, as seeing Him Who is invisible.

Through faith he kept the passover, and the sprinkling of blood, lest he that destroyed the firstborn should touch them.

By faith they passed through the Red sea as by dry *land*: which the Egyptians assaying to do were drowned.

By faith the walls of Jericho fell down, after they were compassed about seven days.

By faith the harlot Rahab perished not with them that believed not, when she had received the spies with peace.

And what shall I more say? for the time would fail me to tell of Gideon, and of Barak, and *of* Samson, and *of* Jephthae; *of* David also, and Samuel, and *of* the prophets:

Who through faith subdued kingdoms, wrought righteousness, obtained promises, stopped the mouths of lions,

Quenched the violence of fire, escaped the edge of the sword, out of weakness were made strong, waxed valiant in fight, turned to flight the armies of the aliens.

Women received their dead raised to life again: and others were tortured, not accepting deliverance; that they might obtain a better resurrection:

And others had trial of *cruel* mockings and scourging, yea, moreover of bonds and imprisonment.

They were stoned, they were sawn asunder, were tempted, were slain with the sword: they wandered about in sheepskins and goatskins; being destitute, afflicted, tormented:

(Of whom the world was not worthy: ) they wandered in deserts, and in mountains, and *in* dens and caves of the earth.

And these all, having obtained a good report through faith, received not the promise,

God having provided some better thing for us, that they without us should not be made perfect.

Hebrews 11:1-40

Each of the courses of believing listed in Hebrews, chapter 11 has its own lessons of finishing. All believing hearts should go back and learn from them. These are believing hearts who won the war of the mind, pulling down the strongholds of unbelief in their believing hearts and fainted not. They weren't perfect but they were faithful. Jesus Christ is the only believing heart who finished, having never followed a course of believing of this world. However, all believing hearts including Jesus, relied upon God's grace and mercy.

The believing hearts of Hebrews, chapter 11 resisted the devil and the devil had to flee. These are believing hearts that became fully persuaded that what God promises he will perform. They staggered not at the promises of God and by patience and endurance inherited the promises of God.

> That ye be not slothful, but followers of them who through faith and patience inherit the promises.
>
> Hebrews 6:12

Jesus provided the greatest example of what it means to inherit the promises of God. His example along with the finishers of Hebrews, chapter 11 provide God's knowledge, wisdom, and understanding, on how to finish a course of believing set by God. Each example has its own specific lessons of how the course was run, how to patiently endure, how to inherit God's promises, and most importantly, how to finish strong.

## The Law of Believing (The Positive Side)

### *Motive: Love of God*

### Run the Course set By God

### *Patiently Endure by Joy and Hope*

### Inherit God's Promises—Finish Strong

"It is finished", are the greatest words that can come out of the mouth of the believing heart. These were the last words spoken by Jesus just before he died on the cross. These were the same words that focused Apostle Paul's life. Joy and hope get the believing heart to the finish. Jesus endured the cross for the joy set before him. Paul finished his course for the hope of Christ's return and the rewards that would follow. These qualities are also found in the finishers in Hebrews, chapter 11. These finishers are God's great cloud of witnesses that surround our believing hearts and demonstrate that it is possible to finish His course. These are the examples God has called us to follow. Examples that lived by believing, inherited his promises, and finished.

# CHAPTER 10

# DEATH IS AN ENEMY

D eath is an enemy to all believing hearts. Eternal death is the ultimate enemy against the believing heart that is not saved. For believing hearts who are saved, premature physical death is the greatest enemy. Premature death cuts short a course that otherwise had more work to be done, more rewards to be gained and more light and life to be brought into this world by the power of God. Once all rule, and all authority, and all power has been delivered to the kingdom of God, then death shall be destroyed.

> But now is Christ risen from the dead, *and* become the first fruits of them that slept.
>
> For since by man *came* death, by man *came* also the resurrection of the dead.
>
> For as in Adam all die, even so in Christ shall all be made alive.
>
> But every man in his own order: Christ the first fruits; afterward they that are Christ's, at His coming.
>
> Then *cometh* the end, when He shall have delivered up the kingdom to God, even the Father; when He shall have put down all rule and all authority and power.

> For He must reign, till He hath put all ene-
> mies under His feet.
> The last enemy *that* shall be destroyed *is* death.

> 1 Corinthians 15:20-26

Death is a constant reminder of the power the devil has, as god of this world. The devil received this power immediately following Adam and Eve's first sin. Since that time, mankind has been subject to the bondage that death brings.

> Forasmuch then as the children are partakers of flesh and blood, He also Himself likewise took part of the same; that through death He might destroy him that had the power of death, that is, the devil; And deliver *them* who through fear of death all their lifetime subject to bondage.

> Hebrews 2:14

Jesus Christ has redeemed mankind from the power of death and destroyed the devil. This victory is only in part in this world. In the next world to come, this victory will be complete.

> And God shall wipe away all tears from their eyes; and there shall be no more death, neither sorrow, nor crying, neither shall there be any more pain: for the former things are passed away."

> Revelation 21:4

As god of this world, the devil is always looking to take advantage of the ignorance of his devices that resides within the believing heart. This is how he keeps some believing hearts from being saved, and cutting short those courses that otherwise would shine in this world. God does not want Satan to have this advantage, and this is why he instructs the believing heart to not be ignorant of Satan's devices.

> Lest Satan should get an advantage of us: for we are not ignorant of his devices.
>
> 2 Corinthians 2:11

The Bible is all about teaching the believing heart how not to be ignorant of Satan's devices. One book that stands out amongst all the rest is the book of Job. Job's master believing heart is matched up against these devices. Revealing the lengths the devil will go to energize his power of death on those who live by believing. It shows how the love of God within the believing heart can prevail over hate and the power of death of this world. When the love of God truly becomes your greatest treasure, you will find the strength to patiently endure all the attacks of the devil, and finish the course set by God. The book of Job also demonstrates how much power the devil has, as god of this world. Signifying his tactics and strategies of steal, kill, and destroy on those believing hearts to which he has access. It reveals his hatred for those who retain the love of God as their mission statement for life. No other book in The Bible goes beyond the law of believing like the book of Job. It takes the believing heart behind the curtain of the spirit world, revealing the two great spiritual powers behind the spiritual power that is energized into this world, God and the devil.

The book of Job begins by giving a reflection of the great treasures of God's Word held within his believing heart. This allowed the power of God to work in his believing heart at a master's level. This was how God was able to bless Job above and beyond what he could ask or think.

> There was a man in the land of Uz, whose name *was* Job; and that man was perfect and upright, and one that feared[biblically, fear in this usage means respect] God, and eschewed evil.
>
> And there were born unto him seven sons and three daughters.
>
> His substance also was seven thousand sheep, and three thousand camels, and five hundred yoke of oxen, and five hundred she asses, and a very great household; so that this man was the greatest of all the men of the east.
>
> Job 1:1-3

At this point, Job is following a course of believing set by God. The power of God emanating from his believing heart was not only visible for all the world to see, but the spirit world was watching.

> And his sons went and feasted *in their* houses, every one his day; and sent and called for their three sisters to eat and to drink with them.
>
> And it was so, when the days of *their* feasting were gone about, that Job sent and sanctified them, and rose early in the morning, and offered

burnt offerings *according* to the number of them all: for Job said, "It may be that my sons have sinned, and cursed God in their hearts." Thus did Job continually.

Job 1:4,5

This is the point in time where Job's believing heart and course of believing is under an evil attack brought on by Satan. Job is concerned for all his sons, that they may have sinned and cursed God in their hearts. This is a serious offense. Biblically, this can lead to becoming an unforgivable sin, risking eternal death. Job said, "It may be that my sons have sinned." He offered burnt offerings according to the number of his sons continually. This means at a minimum, Job worried a lot about his sons. Worry is a devise of Satan to be aware of. At some point this worry grew into fear, which is unbelief. It was at this point where Job's believing changed from a course set by God to the middle section of the law of believing, God's grace and mercy. A course where the only thing that keeps you alive is your love for God, while allowing Satan access into your life. Believing hearts with unbelief are like accidents waiting to happen.

Confidence in an unfaithful man in time of trouble *is like* a broken tooth, and a foot out of joint.

Proverbs 25:19

A broken tooth or a foot out of joint is the description of a believing heart in the middle section of the law of believing. This is what a believing heart mixed with unbelief looks like spiritually. When needed most, it cannot supply strength, and in contrast, it can cause great pain and suffering.

## The Law of Believing (God's Grace and Mercy, The Middle Section)

### *Motivation: Love of God*

### *Positve/Negative Believing*

### Positive and Negative Results, The Power of Death is Held in Abeyance

Unbelief grows hate in the believing heart that works to prevail over the love of God. It's at this point that Job became spiritually blinded, and a course of believing set by the devil was about to begin.

> For the thing which I greatly feared is come upon me, and that which I was afraid of is come unto me.

> Job 3:25

At the end of Job chapter 3, Job recognizes this evil treasure that has corrupted his believing heart. Unfortunately, Job does not see how to recover himself out of this snare of the devil. Job chapters 1 and 2 record the consequences of his unbelief, which energized the power of the devil into this world. Job's example gives a glimpse of the spirit world that goes beyond the law of believing. It reveals great truth about what is actually taking place in the spirit world between God and the devil.

Now there was a day when the sons of God came to present themselves before the L0RD, and Satan came also among them.

And the L0RD said unto Satan, "Whence comest thou?" Then Satan answered the L0RD, and said, "From going to and fro in the earth, and from walking up and down in it."

And the L0RD said unto Satan, "Hast thou considered My servant Job, that *there is* none like him in the earth, a perfect and upright man, one that feareth God, and escheweth evil?"

Then Satan answered the L0RD, and said, "Doth Job fear God for nought?

Hast not *Thou* made an hedge about him, and about his house, and about all that he hath on every side? Thou has blessed the work of his hands, and his substance is increased in the land.

But put forth Thine hand now, and touch all that he hath, and He will curse Thee to They face."

And the L0RD said unto Satan, "Behold, all that he hath *is* in thy power; only upon himself put not forth thine hand."

Job 1:6-12

Only the Word of God can provide this inside look into the spirit world. When Job's believing was on a course set by God, the power of God in the form of prosperity and health magnified in his life. When set on a course by Satan, everything in Job's life was open to attack, except for his own life. Unbelief had grown hate in his believing heart, but not to the point of prevailing. His believing was in the middle section of the law of believing, God's grace and mercy. The greatest treasure of his believing heart, the love of God, was keeping him alive. However, Job's unbelief transferred everything he had to the power of Satan.

> And there was a day when his sons and his daughters *were* eating and drinking wine in their eldest brother's house:
>
> And there came a messenger unto Job, and said, "The oxen were plowing, and the asses feeding beside them: And the Sabeans fell *upon them*, and took them away; yea, they have slain the servants with the edge of the sword; and *I* only am escaped alone to tell thee."
>
> While he *was* yet speaking, there came also another, and said, "The fire of God is fallen from heaven, and hath burned up the sheep, and the servants, and consumed them; and *I* only am escaped alone to tell thee."
>
> While he *was* yet speaking, there came also another, and said, "The Chaldeans made out three bands, and fell upon the camels, and have carried them away, yea, and slain the servants with the edge of the sword; and *I* only am escaped alone to tell thee."
>
> While he *was* yet speaking, there came also another, and said, "Thy sons and thy daughters *were* eating and drinking wine in their eldest brothers house:
>
> And, behold, there came a great wind from the wilderness, and smote the four corners of the house, and it fell upon the young men, and they are dead ; and *I* only am escaped alone to tell thee."

> Then Job arose, and rent his mantle, and
> shaved his head, and fell down upon the ground,
> and worshipped, And said, "Naked came I out
> of my mother's womb, and naked shall I return
> thither: the LORD gave, and the LORD hath taken
> away; blessed be the name of the LORD."
>
> In all this Job sinned not, nor charged God
> foolishly.

Job 1:13-22

All this great evil brought on by Satan, represents two things. Number one, just how much power he has as god of this world. Number two, what he thought it would take for hate to prevail in Job's believing heart. Satan's objective was to end Job's life prematurely. When Satan learned he has miscalculated and still has access to Job's life, he stays on point with this objective. He continued to bring as much evil necessary for hate to prevail in Job's believing heart.

> Again there was a day when the sons of God came
> to present themselves before the LORD, and Satan
> came also among them to present himself before
> the LORD.
>
> And the LORD said unto Satan, "From
> whence comest thou?" And Satan answered the
> LORD, and said, "From going to and fro in the
> earth, and from walking up and down in it."
>
> And the LORD said unto Satan, "Hast thou
> considered My servant Job, that *there is* none like
> him in the earth, a perfect and an upright man, one
> that feareth God, and escheweth evil? And still he
> holdeth fast his integrity, although movedst Me
> aginst him, to destroy him without cause."

And Satan answered the LORD, and said, Skin for skin, yea, all that a man hath will he give for his life. But put forth Thine hand now, and touch his bone and his flesh, and he will curse Thee to Thy face."

And the LORD said unto Satan, "Behold, he *is* in thine hand; but save his life."

So went Satan forth from the presence of the LORD, and smote Job with sore boils from the sole of his foot unto his crown.

And he took him a potsherd to scrape himself withal; and *he* sat down among the ashes.

Then said his wife unto him, "Dost thou still retain thine integrity? Curse God, and die."

But he said unto her, "Thou speakest as one of the foolish women speaketh.

What? shall we receive good at the hand of God, and shall we not receive evil?" In all this did not Job sin with his lips.

Job 2:1-10

Satan thought that boils from the sole of Job's foot to the top of his head would be enough for hate to prevail in Job's believing heart. Satan was wrong again. The love of God within Job's believing heart acts as a wall of fire, protecting Job's life.

For *I*, saith the LORD, will be unto her a wall of fire round about, and will be the glory in the midst of her.

Zechariah 2:5

However, Satan is not through with Job. The remaining chapters of the book of Job record Satan's final attacks on Job's believing heart by three of his friends, and one outsider. The three friends Eliphaz the Tamanite, Bildad the Shuhite, Zophar the Naamathite came first. After they failed, Satan sent Elihu to finish off Job, but Elihu also failed. Through all these attacks Job retained his love for God, and refused to allow hate to prevail in his believing heart. By chapter 42 Job has identified the unbelief in his believing heart, and confesses his sin before God, putting his believing back on a course set by God.

> Then Job answered the LORD, and said, "I know that Thou canst do every*thing*, and *that* no thought can be withholden from Thee.
>
> Who *is* he that hideth counsel without knowledge? therefore have I uttered that I understood not; things too wonderful for me, which I know not.
>
> Hear, I beseech Thee, and *I* will speak: I will demand of thee, and declare thou unto me.
>
> I have heard of Thee by the hearing of the ear: but now mine eye seeth Thee.
>
> Wherefore I abhor *myself*, and repent [biblically, repent means to change the heart] in dust and ashes."
>
> Job 42:1-6

Job repented from the course of evil he had been following, and changed his believing heart to follow a course set by God. He retained his love for God and refused for hate to prevail in his believing heart. He refused to cross the line of the law of believing to the negative side and allow Satan to take his life. He would not allow himself to be ignorant of this device of Satan.

## The Law of Believing

(The Positive Side) | (God's Grace and Mercy) | (The Negative Side)

| *Love of God* | *Love of God* | *Hate* |
| --- | --- | --- |
| *Believing* | *Believing/Unbelief* | *Unbelief* |

Power of God | Power God—Power of Devil | Power of Devil

Death Held in Abeyance

Job's greatest treasure, the love of God was a wall of fire about his life that never failed. Job got back on God's course, back to his master believing heart level, and finished his course in believing.

> So the LORD blessed the latter end of Job more than his beginning: for he had fourteen thousand sheep, and six thousand camels, and a thousand yoke of oxen, and a thousand she asses.
>
> He had also seven sons and three daughters. And he called the name of the first Jemima; and name of the second, Kezia; and the name of the third, Keren-happuch.
>
> And in all the land were no women *so* fair as the daughters of Job: and their father gave them inheritance among the brethren.
>
> After this lived Job an hundred and forty years, and saw his sons, and his sons' sons, *even* four generations.
>
> So Job died, being old and full of days.
>
> Job 42:12-17

Death is an enemy to all believing hearts. Eternal death is the greatest enemy to those who have not made Jesus Lord. For believing hearts that are saved, premature death is an enemy. It cuts short a course that otherwise has more work to be done, more rewards to be gained, and more light and life to be brought into this world, by the power of God. The devil has the power of death in this world. In the next world to come, the devil and the power of death shall be no more. Job recognized death was an enemy and he fought Satan off by retaining his integrity, which was his love for God. The book of Job shows how the spirit world is always paying attention to the treasures of the believing heart. God and Satan, who are of the spirit world, are the real powers of this world. These powers are at work beyond the law of believing, which energize the believing heart. Both powers desire for their power to enter this world. Both powers are subject to the law of believing. Satan is going to take calculated guesses to manipulate the future of weak believing hearts, while God knows all. Satan knows who lives by believing and those who are spiritually blind, those upon whom he can inflict great evil, and those he can't. God protects those who live by believing. Before Job sinned, God was able to prosper and protect his life from the power of the devil. The love of God built deeply into Job's believing heart was a wall of fire that kept Satan from taking his life after he sinned. Satan was continuously wrong about Job, but this did not stop his relentless attacks on his life. Only when Job confessed his sin before God, did his believing heart become energized by the power of God, turning back the spiritual captivity held by Satan. This is how Satan's attacks are completely stopped. As god of this world, he has the right to attack throughout a course of believing, but not to win. This part of Job's life made him wiser and stronger. He didn't get tricked by Satan again. Job returned to a new course set by God, a course which he finished being *old and full of days*. His latter end was truly greater than his beginning. This is God's will for all believing hearts: a long, healthy, and prosperous life, becoming the wise man, just like Job.

# CONCLUSION

Thank you for reading *Treasures of the Believing Heart*. My sincere desire is that the Bible becomes more than just a book: that it becomes God's Word, written just for you to live by believing. That from this day forward and the rest of your life, "It is Finished" focuses your life and that you will receive a full reward at Christ's return. Thank you and may God bless your life abundantly, above all you can ask or think, according to the energized power of God that will work in you as you believe.

For more information or to contact me please visit my website treasuresofthebelievingheart@tateauthor.com or follow me on Facebook and Twitter.

> For all flesh *is* as grass, and all the glory of man as the flower of grass. The grass withereth, and the flower thereof falleth away:
>
> But the word of the LORD endureth for ever. And this is the word which by the gospel is preached unto you.
>
> Wherefore laying aside all malice, and all guile, and hypocrisies, and envies, and all evil speakings,
>
> As newborn babes, desire the sincere milk of the word, that ye may grow thereby:
>
> If so be ye have tasted that the LORD *is* gracious.
>
> I Peter 1:24-25; 2:1-3

Now unto Him That is able to keep you from falling, and to present *you* faultless before the presence of His glory with exceeding joy,

To the only wise God our Savior, *be* glory and majesty, dominion and power, now and ever. Amen.

Jude 1:24,25

# BIBLIOGRAPHY

Alchin, L.K. *Roman Colosseum*. Retrieved November 10th, 2010. *www.roman.colusseum.info*

*The Companion Bible*. Grand Rapids, Michigan: Kregel Publications, 1990.